Shipping Practice

Shipping Practice

With a consideration of the relevant law

Eleventh Edition

Edward F Stevens FICS, FCIS
and **C S J Butterfield** FICS, FIFF, MCIT, ACIArb

with a Foreword by the late Lord Essendon

Pitman

PITMAN BOOKS LIMITED
128 Long Acre, WC2E 9AN

PITMAN PUBLISHING INC
1020 Plain Street, Marshfield, Massachusetts

Associated Companies
Pitman Publishing Pty Ltd, Melbourne
Pitman Publishing New Zealand Ltd, Wellington
Copp Clark Pitman, Toronto

Printed and bound in Great Britain
at The Pitman Press, Bath

ISBN 0–273–01616–4

Contents

Foreword

By the late Lord Essendon

The business of shipowning is one of the most complex of all the industrial occupations. It has romance to recommend it, and it is never-ending in the presentation of problems which are not merely new in themselves but also have a great variety of different angles. It is therefore most important that the student of shipowning should secure a firm grasp of the fundamentals, and *Shipping Practice* is a valuable addition to the student's library.

No textbook of reasonable dimensions could possibly cover the ground completely, and no textbook could take the place of practical experience, but *Shipping Practice* will give the student a very fair idea and knowledge of the wide range of subjects which are involved in the running of ships under modern conditions.

ESSENDON

Preface
to Tenth Edition

It is an essential duty of individuals today to be conversant with the business in which they are occupied.

This book is written to guide the student through the various and extensive subjects connected with Shipping, without a deep treatment of the law, and the compilation has been arranged in a progressive order of study, and, as far as is possible within the scope of the volume, covers the necessary subjects for the Institute of Chartered Shipbrokers, Chartered Institute of Transport, Institute of Export, London Chamber of Commerce, and Royal Society of Arts Examinations. It is pleasing to note that since its original edition this volume has been approved by many Institutes and Organizations as a recommended book for study.

Whilst primarily its object is that of a textbook for the student, it is hoped that it will prove of benefit and contain interesting details and information for others engaged in this profession, perhaps leading many to make a more extensive study of 'Shipping'. It is felt timely to mention that the considerable volume of recent and pending Legislation, as it may affect shipping matters, requires of students a continuous study of such new Law to keep up to date with the changes brought about by fresh Acts and/or Statutory Orders made under them.

Acknowledgments and sincere thanks are due to the following bodies who have kindly permitted various documents to be reproduced – Blue Funnel Line, Manchester Liners Ltd, Lloyd's Register of Shipping, The General Council of British Shipping, Corporation of Lloyd's and HMSO for permission to reproduce the text of the Carriage of Goods by Sea Act 1971.

To Mr L. T. J. Reynolds, M.I.N., A.M.I.Ex., I.S.F.A. Dip., Director of Studies, Shipping and Transport Division, Thurrock Technical College, for providing the chapter on Containerization.

And, to Mr C. S. J. Butterfield, F.I.C.S., M.C.I.T., A.I.Arb., who has undertaken the revision of this edition.

E.F.S.

Preface

to Eleventh Edition

Since my old friend and colleague E. F. Stevens produced the first edition of *Shipping Practice* in 1935 the shipping industry has gone through many changes, not the least of these being the emergence of the giant bulk carriers and the onset of containerization. There has also been a vast amount of legislation dealing directly or obliquely with the industry and it is to be hoped that the industry will have time to digest it.

Honoured names have gone either by amalgamation or other means, but the industry continues to develop with fresh trades and new techniques, and these pose a challenge to all.

This textbook is directed at young students of shipping affairs and is intended to act as an elementary guide through their studies of one of the most involved yet most interesting industries that exist.

My sincere thanks are accorded to Manchester Liners Ltd, Ben Ocean Joint Service, Lloyd's Register of Shipping, the General Council of British Shipping; the Institute of Chartered Shipbrokers; the Chartered Institute of Arbitrators; to Mr W. G. Raper, Director of Overseas Containers (Europe) Ltd, and Mr L. T. J. Reynolds, M.B.E., M.I.N., A.M.I.Ex., I.S.F.A.Dip., Director of Studies, Shipping and Transport Division, Thurrock Technical College, for the chapter on containerization, and to HMSO for permission to reproduce the text of the Carriage of Goods by Sea Act 1971.

C.S.J.B.

1 The Shipping Company

Shipping companies are organized for the purpose of running direct lines and regular services between certain ports, or for the purpose of owning vessels which may be chartered as and when business is offered. Reference to chartering is made in a special chapter, and here it is necessary to consider only the work and organization of a liner shipping company.

The term *liner* does not necessarily include only a large vessel of the *Queen Elizabeth 2* type, but includes any vessel which regularly runs on a service between certain ports. A *tramp* ship is one which sails here and there, picking up business on its course; many so-called tramp ships are better equipped and in better condition than some 'liners'.

The shipping company, having determined where they intend to develop a service, arrange for a number of vessels to serve the selected route, making weekly, fortnightly, or other periodic calls according to the cargo which may be offered.

It is the duty of the company in their own interest to provide speedy and safe vessels, keeping them fit for a continuous service. As a matter of interest, it may be observed that many companies purchase new vessels from time to time and place them on the service together with their older vessels; but it is not practical to run the new vessels at a greater speed than the old, otherwise the regularity of the service would become disorganized.

Having in mind the necessity for replacements in order to retain trade in competitive markets, the shipping company should provide for depreciation in order that their vessels may continuously be brought up to date and modernized. Striking examples have been seen where companies have retained old ships and never made replacements until eventually their business has completely dwindled away and their ships have become valueless. Strict rules cannot be laid down in this connection. The ship-owner has to ensure that due to the extremely high cost of modern and up-to-date vessels, these must be fully occupied in order to bring an equitable return over the years on the capital sum invested. To do so liner companies frequently rationalize sailings with their competitors.

When the shipping company has decided to commence a service, advertisements of sailings are regularly made, sailing cards sent to merchants and agents, and canvassers appointed to secure the necessary business. This notification to shippers is not the *offer* of the contract of affreightment as mentioned in the chapter on 'Bills of Lading'. The shipper on sending goods down to the vessel makes his offer, which is accepted by the shipowner when the goods are shipped. Thus the shutting out of cargo by a ship is no breach of contract.

Where 'registration schemes' operate, the registration by the shipper must be deemed his offer of cargo, and the drawing off by the shipowner as the acceptance of the contract.

The date when a ship ceased to load cargo is shown on the sailing card, and known as the *closing date*. Up to such time the ship will receive and load cargo. The words originated from the earlier expression in sailing ship days, as the intended date when the ship closed her hatches preparatory to sailing.

The procedure now described would apply in the case of a conventional vessel, loading an assorted general cargo. The goods are received by the ship in two ways, either *alongside* or into a *shed*. When goods are received into shed a *dock receipt* or wharfinger's receipt is given for such goods, and the goods are retained in the shed until required for loading.

This receipt is now issued by a Standard Shipping Note, which is required by a number of ports and is accepted by all UK ports. It must accompany all export cargo to the dock or ship for alongside delivery. This Standard Shipping Note contains a counterfoil which when signed serves as a dock receipt. When goods are received alongside, a *mate's receipt* for water-borne cargo is given. For water-borne cargo a Standard Shipping Note can be used or if the lightman requires it a mate's receipt can still be obtained. (In view of the reduction of conventional loading and of the lighterage of export cargo, it may not be long before the 'mate's receipt' lapses.)

When mate's receipts are issued the shipping company will not issue bills of lading until such time as the mate's receipt is given in exchange. The reason for this is that the mate's receipt is signed by the chief officer of the ship, consequently the bill of lading which is also a receipt for goods should not be issued until this temporary receipt (mate's receipt) is returned.

The question of the liability of the company for issuing bills of lading without requiring the mate's receipt to be given up is in an unsatisfactory state. In the case of *Schuster* v. *M'Kellar* (1857), 26 L.J.Q.B. 281, Lord Campbell left the question to the jury whether under the peculiar circumstances of that case the master was justified 'in obtaining and putting the signature to the bill of lading ... without the production of the mate's receipt'. The jury held that he was not. On the other hand it has been held that the master of a vessel may sign bills of lading in favour of the shipper of goods without production of the mate's receipt, if he is satisfied otherwise that the goods are on board, and if he has no notice that anyone but the shipper claims any interest in them (*Hathesing* v. *Laing* (1873), L.R. 17 Eq. 92). In the same case the court expressed the opinion that the mate's receipt was assignable, only, as in the case of any other chose in action, notice of the assignment was necessary to bind the shipowner.

When a shipper has a large quantity of cargo which he is desirous of sending by a special vessel, he will approach the company to book space. Also when such cargo as he is sending is of a dangerous or inflammable nature or requiring special care he will obtain a stowage order for these goods.

Goods are tallied into the vessel by tally clerks, whose duty is to keep a check and list of all cargo stowed in the vessel.

Tallying is done by recording in books, on cards, or on sheets, the mark, port, numbers, and number of packages, with any remarks regarding condition.

The process of tallying is essentially one with which great care should be taken. Many cases arise where owing to a wrong tally, bills of lading are issued for goods which have never been shipped. When bills of lading are issued in this manner, the consignee on failing to receive his cargo at port of delivery holds a document of title and has every right to claim the full value of his cargo although same was never shipped. The carrier must, in order to secure freedom from liability, prove that the goods were never on board, which may entail great inconvenience and also be very difficult.

Against the particulars of the packages on the tally cards, are the measurements and weight by which freight is charged. Any disputed weights may be checked at port of delivery, and it found to be incorrect, checking charges are for account of carrier. If, however, the original weight or measurement is found to be correct the charge for this checking is for account of the person requiring the check.

As goods are tallied into the ship, so the tally cards are sent to the shipping company's office. These are divided into ports, each port being controlled by a port clerk, whose duty is to check the particulars on the bill of lading with those on the tally card. When the shipment shown on a bill of lading is received on board, the bill of lading is signed and the particulars are placed on the ship's manifest. This manifest must contain full particulars of marks, numbers, quantity, contents, shipper, and consignee, with particulars required by the consular authorities of the country to which the goods are being forwarded.

The freight account is made out and freight is chargeable according to weight or measurement, or *ad valorem* value, whichever may be the most remunerative to the carrier. In addition to freight there may be charges for forwarding, clearance, and sometimes a charge for primage.

Conferences of the different trades are organized whereby all shipping companies trading in certain areas meet and discuss matters of general interest, compile tariffs of rates for specific goods, and generally control and protect the interest of all members. In order to ensure that the shippers by conference lines maintain their support in return for the regular services provided, a primage charge of varying amounts up to 10 per cent is charged on the total freight. This is retained by the shipping

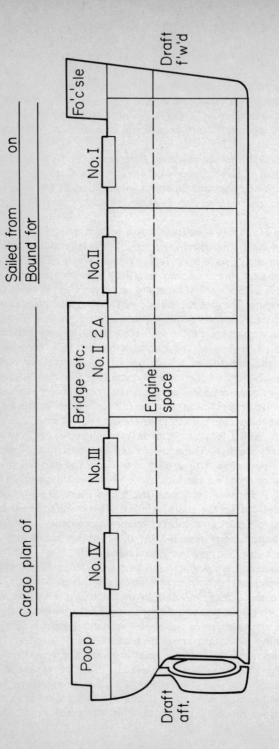

Cargo plan of _____

Sailed from _____ on _____

Bound for _____

Draft f'w'd

Fo'c'sle

No. I

No. II

Bridge etc.
No. II 2A

Engine space

No. III

No. IV

Poop

Draft aft.

Note
Normally cargo plans are not less than 2 ft in length.

company for a period of three or six months, and is then returnable as rebate to the shipper, provided that during that period he has not forwarded goods to the same area by any vessel other than a conference boat. Or, the contract system is used, whereby primage is dropped and the regular shipper gets a 'contract rate' which is lower than the rate charged to a shipper who does not sign a contract to ship only by conference vessels.

One copy of the manifest and a plain copy of each bill of lading, known as the captain's copy, is forwarded to the port of delivery. Other copies of manifests and bills of lading are handed to customs and consular authorities as required.

On arrival of the vessel at the port of destination, the consignee presents his bill of lading to the shipping company, or their local representatives, who issue a delivery order in exchange, which the consignee hands to the officer in charge of the ship and obtains his cargo.

In order to avoid delay in sorting cargo on arrival, stowage plans are made out by the loading staff which show the position of the goods. In this manner, and by this guide, each receiver of cargo is advised where his cargo is, when it will be delivered, and consequently delay and time lost awaiting cargo is diminished.

An example of a stowage plan is shown on page 4; the position of cargo as loaded has to be inserted thereon.

In stowing cargoes the stevedores see that all light cargoes are stowed over heavy cargoes, and that protection is made, by way of dunnage mats, or alternatives, for separating the cargo.

Much space is lost in stowing packages of irregular shape such as barrels, drums, awkward shaped cases, etc., and this space is termed broken stowage. It must not be confused with the term *breaking bulk*, which is the expression used for opening a hatch at port of delivery and removing cargo.

Shipments under charter-parties are very similar. The carrier provides the vessel according to the charter-party terms, and the charterer supplies the cargo to the ship as fast as she can load. This cargo is tallied into the ship, or when the shipment is a bulk cargo the amount supplied is said to be so many tons upon which freight is charged. The method of tallying and preparation of ship's papers is identical, although in charter-party shipments usually one or only a few bills of lading are issued compared with perhaps 200 to 400 bills under a berth contract.

2 The Shipowner and Merchant

A merchant, manufacturer, or agent seeking business overseas must generally use the sea as a principal means of transport to his market.

His business development depends upon the cheapness of the cost of transportation, coupled with a reliable and regular service. A comparison of railway rates and coastal transport rates shows a big difference in cost in dealing with home trade.

When by a very small increase in the total cost of transportation a market is lost it is the duty of the shipper to secure the cheapest method of transportation. Sea carrying is in many trades divided into two sections, viz. mail ships, and slow ships, and a small increase in rate is sometimes made for carriage of goods by the faster vessel. For a steady supply to markets the merchant may take advantage of the lower cost, or when necessity demands the speedy arrival of the goods at their destination, then he may resort to the faster vessels at a small additional charge.

Merchants who deal in small shipments avail themselves of the regular advertised lines which receive cargo on the berth and maintain weekly or fortnightly services. If, however, the merchant is a dealer in large quantity shipments then he has the option of chartering a vessel for his own use. Here the comparison between tariff rates and chartered rates shows that the chartered vessel is the cheapest means of transport for bulk cargoes. The shipowner is assured of his earnings, has less trouble in the management of the business, but meets with strict opposition from all other chartering brokers and owners. Consequently chartered rates are competitive and fluctuate from high rates when tonnage is scarce, to low rates when tonnage is freely available.

Transportation by air has in recent years increased rapidly, and shipping companies feel the competition for the small, highly valuable consignments, but not for bulk carrying because of the aircraft's relatively low capacity. Consideration of the point of how many air liners would be required to transport a cargo of, say, 15,000 tons gives ample proof of this. However, the fact must not be lost sight of that for fast transport of small and important cargoes aircraft carriage has established a definite place.

The shipowner as a public carrier obtains his living from the business secured by the merchants in foreign markets, and he is the first to suffer in times of depression due to diminution of trade. While he runs his service firstly for his own benefit and profit, much of his time is spent in seeking ways of improvement for the benefit of his shippers.

The carrier or shipowner realizes that co-ordination with the merchant is essential, not only for his own business but for that of the merchant, and we find the owners of the individual trades co-operating with one another to secure the satisfaction of all their clients.

The shipping conferences of the different trades are an illustration of this co-operative movement. The River Plate, South African, and Australian conferences, to mention a few, are committees of representatives of all owners interested in these particular areas. They meet to consider their joint interests, establish freight rates, and deal in all matters of importance.

While they run regular services of benefit to merchants, they in return expect the merchant to co-operate with them to make possible and ensure these steady sailings, and they accordingly demand a guarantee from all shippers of their continued support. As already stated in the previous chapter, primage is charged by many conferences, which is a deposit returnable after a stated period provided that during such time the shipper has not shipped by lines other than conference lines, any failure to give continued support rendering the shipper liable to lose his rebate at the end of that period. Or the contract system may be used.

In support of this pressure, which may at first sight appear arbitrary, it may be stated that since the shipowner operates a service of good vessels with regularity irrespective of good or bad trade, if a vessel of an opposition owner is placed in competition at a lower rate of freight to secure occasional business, he should not suffer by this casual opposition in order that the shipper may sometimes be financially slightly better off.

Whilst the shipping conferences set rates and compile tariffs for the trades in which they deal, they are always willing to consider the case when a rate may appear to be strangling the endeavours of a merchant in securing business in a foreign market. If for example a merchant finds that, with the cost of his article plus the freight charged, he is, for a small sum per article unable to compete with foreign merchants, then, by application to the conference of that particular trade, he may, on proving that by a reduction of freight rates he has good prospects of obtaining a ready sale, secure a suitable reduction in rate, provided he can satisfy the conference of his ability to ship an assured quantity.

In addition to the foregoing, where a line is being run under conference agreement, the shipper is able to quote rates for forward shipments, knowing the cost of transportation, and has no fear that he will suffer loss in this connection.

The shipping companies also provide co-ordination with the shippers by the provision of additional departments for the purpose of forwarding and insurance, thus not only supplementing their own profit by increased business, but also giving to the shipper the advantage that if he so desires he may carry out the whole of his forwarding business through one organization. The shipper knows that here is a qualified and well organized staff ready at his disposal to arrange the shipment of his goods, see to the whole of the forwarding, insure the goods under the best cover at the most reasonable rate, and carry out any other duties he may desire.

The section of transit that the shipowner is concerned with is the portion from the time of loading on board his vessel to the time of discharge, but here again he will arrange for transhipment at either end of the voyage in question under what are known as 'through bills of lading'.

3 The Merchant Shipper

The business activities of the merchant shipper are nearly as multitudinous as those of the shipowner. He must have an intimate knowledge of the requirements of the markets of the world, and the realization of the right goods for particular areas.

He supplies his own branches abroad with manufactured stock or forwards goods according to the order he may receive from his clients. He may deal as buying agent for overseas clients, in which case he receives either open or closed orders. The closed orders are orders for specific goods of a certain manufacture, in which case the merchant shipper arranges the purchase accordingly. If, however, he received an open order he makes inquiries in the corresponding markets and obtains suitable goods at the most reasonable prices.

Having obtained the goods he arranges for the packing to be done. This in itself is work for an expert. Much money can be saved by the manner in which goods are packed. The packer must have a knowledge of the rates of freight chargeable on goods, and must see that no high rated goods are packed with low rated goods. It is the custom and right of the shipping companies to charge freight at the highest rate on goods contained in a case. If, therefore, a packer packs a case of tin saucepans which may be rated £5.00 and includes in the case a package of silk goods which are rated at say £10.00 then irrespective of the fact that the saucepans take up 95 per cent of the space of the case the rate of freight chargeable would be £10.00. This additional freight could easily place upon the cost of the saucepans sufficient extra cost to be the cause of a lost market. The packer, therefore, would be better advised to make one case of the saucepans, which would be chargeable at £5.00 and another smaller package of the silk goods chargeable at £10.00, and a saving in freight would then be made.

When the packer has sorted his goods for packing into their nearest selection for rating purposes, he packs the goods. Here again much money may be saved in the method of packing. A great amount of goods exported are now packed in tanks, which are stronger than cases, and which may at port of destination be sold for a small amount thus regaining the cost of the packing.

If wooden cases are strengthened by battens, the case is measured from the edge of the battens, making a few more inches in size, and again producing an increase in freight charges. Here the advantage is to have the cases banded with iron, which, whilst being equally as strong as the wood battens, does not increase the cubic space occupied. With the considerable progress in development of carton packing, the shipowner is compelled to recognize this as a standard form of packaging goods for export, without adding an 'insufficiently packed' clause on his bills of lading.

Much space may be lost through irregular objects being packed. An example of this is shown in the following illustration:

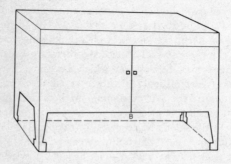

The illustration shows a cabinet packed in a case. The case must be large enough to enclose the whole of the cabinet; it would be folly to attempt to pack the case in any other fashion. Therefore, the space marked 'B' inside the case remains empty, and consequently the shipper has to pay freight on the empty space contained in the case. This adds to the cost of the shipping, and incidentally to the cost of the cabinet when offered for sale in the foreign market.

The packer, therefore, seeking to use this space in the best manner possible, would arrange with the supplier to approach the buyer to take with each cabinet, a few smaller objects. This, if so agreed, provides the necessary cargo which may be stowed in the space 'B', and consequently the other articles are carried by the shipping company without increase of freight.

There is also much development in the use of containers which are used to save packing costs and simplify handling.

When goods are packed the cases must be marked clearly, showing the mark, number, and port of destination. Marks are used purely for identity purposes, but such marking must be made in a clear fashion and in such manner as to remain legible for the whole of the voyage in prospect. Reference to the Carriage of Goods by Sea Act will show that it is the duty of the shipper clearly to mark his cases and he is deemed to guarantee the accuracy of such marks.

Having packed the case the merchant arranges the shipment of the goods, or employs a shipping agent for this purpose. Or again the forwarding department of the shipping company itself may be employed for this service. As all operate in a similar fashion we will assume the merchant arranges his own shipment.

He finds a suitable sailing which will fit his requirements and approaches the shipping company with the request for them to book space. If the case requires any special care in regard to stowage, a special stowage order will be issued. The company having agreed to carry the goods will advise the merchant where to send the goods for shipment, giving dock, and date when the vessel is receiving cargo.

The documents are then prepared, and the bills of lading are made out by the merchant shipper. The particulars required are set out in chapter 5. Each country differs in regard to information required in the bill of lading, and the number of bills of lading necessary for the *set*. In addition, certificates of origin are sometimes demanded by the consular authorities. This is a certificate stating the country of origin of the goods shipped, an example of which is given in the appendix.

Should the documents be made out by the shipping agent, or shipping company, the merchant supplies an invoice of the goods showing full particulars, from which information the bills of lading are compiled.

The bills of lading are then handed to the shipping company who retain them until such time as the goods have been *returned* from the docks. This *return* or tally is the notification from the loading staff to the office staff that the goods have been received on board, or received for shipment.

The merchant then keeps in constant touch with the shipping company, and when he ascertains that his bills of lading are awaiting collection, pays freight and takes delivery of his documents.

It is then the duty of the merchant to arrange that the bill of lading is forwarded to his consignee.

When the goods are being forwarded to a branch office the need for financial security is unnecessary, the merchant encloses a bill of lading, certificate of origin (where necessary) and invoice of goods giving details of costs, freight, insurances, packing, and other charges, in an envelope addressed to his consignee, and hands it to the shipping company for inclusion in the ship's mail.

Should the bill of lading be made out in the name of a specific consignee, it does not require to be endorsed, but when the bill is made out in the name of (order) it must be endorsed by the merchant before being sent forward.

The necessity of arranging for the bill of lading to be placed in the ship's mail, is the security that the bill of lading shall be in the hands of the receiver when the goods arrive, thereby preventing delay. If it is possible to forward these documents by a mail ship or airmail, which arrives earlier, giving additional time for clearance arrangements to be made, this has even greater advantages. Some foreign countries levy fines if cargo arrives and no document has been received for its clearance.

In order to ensure the safe arrival of the document, another bill of lading may be forwarded by following mail, or by an alternative route, in case the first bill of lading should be mislaid and cause inconvenience. The legal position in relation to the issue of a first and second bill of lading is referred to under another chapter.

Where a merchant is forwarding goods to a receiver of whom he has little knowledge, or whose financial status is insufficient to give him the desired confidence, he may place the documents through a bank, thus ensuring himself of his charges, and avoiding any sense of insecurity.

The documents are handed to the bankers with bill of exchange, insurance policy, and a letter of hypothecation, in return for which the bank either meets the charges of the invoice, or credits the account of the merchant at a future date.

The letter of hypothecation is, briefly, a document which gives the holder the right, if the charges are not forthcoming or if a bill of exchange has been received and such a bill is dishonoured, to sell the goods on arrival and take the proceeds to recoup him for his advance.

By this method the merchant is assured of his money and has no fear of suffering a loss upon the shipment.

Another method of foreign trade finance is by way of consignment accounts when the merchant here does not sell the goods to the consignee. The consignee receives the goods and arranges for their disposal. Whilst he has them in his possession they still remain the property of the merchant, the consignee acting only as the selling agent at port of destination.

As the goods are sold, entries of such transactions are made in a special account known as the '. . . . . Consignment a/c', and from time to time the receiver forwards to the merchant an account of sales. He receives in return for his services in the disposal of the goods a commission by way of remuneration, the proceeds of the sale being forwarded to the merchant at agreed periods.

To comply with currency regulations and control, the method of shipping goods against bank credits has rapidly become established. The overseas customer issues his order for goods, and arranges a bank credit for payment in the seller's country. Credits are issued as unconfirmed or revocable, irrevocable, confirmed irrevocable, etc.

Shipment on the exact terms of the credit earns payment against documents. The foolish insistence on obscure descriptions and bankers' lack of knowledge of shipping often result in the bank credit system becoming cumbersome and the subject of hot dispute.

On receipt of the bill of lading at the port of destination the consignee, after endorsing the document, presents the bill at the shipping office and secures in return a delivery order, which is an authority to the master of the ship to make delivery of the goods in exchange for this order.

A merchant shipper who uses the chartered ship as his method of transport has considerably less work to do; he has merely to supply the goods in bulk to the vessel, receive payment for the goods, and forward the bill of lading to the consignee. The main difference here is that the consignee or receiver does not usually pay his freight until such time as the goods are discharged. This, however, is dealt with fully in chapters 7 and 8.

4 Limitation of Shipowner's Liability

In order to lessen the liability of a shipowner for damages through loss or injury arising at sea, the legislature has imposed limitations upon the amount which may be recovered in certain actions against a shipowner. These limitations are contained in Sects 502—509 of the Merchant Shipping Act 1894, as amended by subsequent statutes, and the Merchant Shipping (Liability of Shipowners and Others) Act 1958; the provisions of these sections are unaffected by the Carriage of Goods by Sea Act 1971, which, to a certain extent, however, increases the liabilities of the ship-owner by preventing him from contracting out of certain of his defined liabilities (see chapter 6). It is the purpose of this chapter to summarize the provisions of the Merchant Shipping Acts relative to the limitation of the shipowner's liability.

The owner of a British sea-going ship, or any share therein, is not liable to make good to any extent whatever any loss or damage happening *without his actual fault or privity* in the following cases; namely:

(1) Where any goods, merchandise, or other things whatsoever taken in or put on board his ship are lost or damaged by reason of fire on board the ship; or

(2) Where any gold, silver, diamonds, watches, jewels, or precious stones taken in or put on board his ship, the true nature and value of which have not at the time of shipment been declared by the owner or shipper thereof to the owner or master of the ship in the bill of lading or otherwise in writing, are lost or damaged by reason of any robbery, embezzlement, making away with, or secreting thereof.

The owners of a British or foreign ship are not liable beyond certain specified amounts where all or any of the following occurrences take place without their actual fault or privity:

(1) Where any loss of life or personal injury is caused to any person being carried in the ship;

(2) Where any damage or loss is caused to any goods, merchandise, or other things whatsoever on board the ship;

(3) Where any loss of life or personal injury is caused to any person not carried in the ship through the act or omission of any person (whether on board the ship or not) in the navigation or management of the ship or in the loading, carriage or discharge of its cargo in the embarkation, carriage or disembarkation of its passengers, or through any other act or omission of any person on board the ship;

(4) Where any loss or damage is caused to any property (other than any property mentioned in paragraph (2) above) or any rights are infringed through the act or omission of any person (whether on board the ship or not) in the navigation or management of the ship, or in the loading, carriage or discharge of its cargo or in the embarkation, carriage or disembarkation of its passengers, or through any other act or omission of any person on board the ship.

The specified amounts above referred to are as follows:

(1) In respect of loss of life or personal injury, either alone or together with loss of or damage to vessels, goods, merchandise, or other things, an aggregate amount not exceeding 3100 gold francs for each ton of their ship's tonnage; and

(2) In respect of loss of, or damage to, vessels, goods, merchandise, or other things, whether there be in addition loss of life or personal injury or not, an aggregate amount not exceeding 1000 gold francs for each ton of their ship's tonnage.

The tonnage of a vessel is her registered tonnage with the addition of engine room; and the tonnage of a sailing ship is her registered tonnage.

The owner of every sea-going ship or share therein is liable in respect of every such loss of life, personal injury, loss of or damage to vessels, goods, merchandise, or things arising on distinct occasions to the same extent as if no other loss, injury, or damage had arisen.

Where any liability is alleged to have been incurred by the owner of a British or foreign ship in respect of loss of life, personal injury, or loss of or damage to vessels or goods, and several claims are made or apprehended in respect of that liability, then the owner may apply to the High Court to determine the amount of the owner's liability and may distribute that amount rateably among the several claimants, and may stay any proceedings pending in any other court in relation to the same matter, and may proceed in such manner and subject to such regulations as to making persons interested parties to the proceedings, and as to the exclusion of any claimants who do not come in within a certain time, and as to requiring security from the owner, and as to payment of any costs as the court thinks just.

A shipowner may, of course, waive his rights under the statute by special contract.

It may be observed that the usual course when seeking limitation of liability is for the shipowner to pay the sum of 1000 or 3100 gold francs per ton, as the case may be, in Court, and to ask for a decree limiting his liability to that amount.

5 Bills of Lading

The document under which cargo is carried on board vessels is a bill of lading, and may be defined as a receipt for goods, signed by the master or other duly authorized person on behalf of the shipowner, and constitutes a document of title to the goods specified therein.

For over three hundred years, bills of lading have been most important documents in a variety of international trade transactions. Their format has varied in accordance with the particular trade and the requirements of individual shipowners.

Whilst it is primarily a receipt, and not strictly speaking a contract of carriage, it is nevertheless good, and sometimes the only evidence of the terms and conditions of carriage.

There has been some divergence of opinion as to whether a bill of lading is in fact a receipt or a contract, but in the case of *Sewell* v. *Burdick* (1884), 10 App. Cas. 74, Lord Bramwell stated:

> There is I think another inaccuracy in the statute (Bill of Lading Act 1855) which is indeed universal. It speaks of the contract contained in the bill of lading. To my mind there is no contract in it. It is a receipt for goods stating the terms on which they are to be received and carried by the ship, and, therefore, excellent evidence of those terms, but it is not a contract. That has been made before the bill of lading has been given.

The words of his Lordship put the question in its proper perspective and eliminate all doubt.

The indispensable features of every contract are of course *offer* and *acceptance*. When a shipowner advertises his vessel for the carriage of cargo, and the shipper signifies his offer by requesting the owner to reserve space in the vessel, he thereby makes an offer. It is only when the shipowner has accepted the cargo on board that the contract of affreightment is concluded.

It would be as well to explain that if the contract of carriage consisted merely of an unqualified offer and acceptance — without any special terms and conditions of contract — the shipowner would constitute himself a 'common carrier', and would consequently render himself liable for any damage the goods may sustain whilst in his custody, excepting only that attributable to:

16

> Act of God;
> Queen's enemies;
> Inherent vice.

His liability would, however, be limited by the provisions of the Merchant Shipping Acts referred to in chapter 4.

The shipowner is at liberty to restrict his liabilities, and this he seeks to do by concluding special contracts as evidenced by the terms, conditions and exceptions of the bills of lading. A glance at a modern general cargo bill of lading will convince one that the shipowner takes every precaution to minimize his liabilities by inserting protective clauses exempting himself from responsibility for a very exhaustive range of losses, including those arising from the negligence of his servants, etc. Bills of lading for goods shipped from the United Kingdom and Northern Ireland, however, are in this respect subject to the Carriage of Goods by Sea Act 1971, which forms the subject of a separate chapter in this volume.

The act establishes the responsibilities, liabilities, rights and immunities attaching to carriers under bills of lading, and in effect prescribes a standard form of bill of lading which has the force of law. It removes the difficulties and uncertainties which were associated with the plethora of protective clauses which shipowners were accustomed to insert in bills of lading and has bestowed a considerable advantage on the mercantile community, particularly banks and insurance companies, as, now that they know exactly the extent of the shipowners' liabilities, etc., they can make advances and adjust insurance premiums on cargo with greater facility. It is not necessary specifically to incorporate fully the terms and conditions of the Carriage of Goods by Sea Act 1971 in bills of lading.

It is the shipper's duty to supply the shipping company with the bills of lading. As soon as the shipper ascertains the number of packages he wishes to ship by the vessel, he completes the bills of lading and lodges these with the shipping company for their attention.

He may, however, request the carrying company to make out bills of lading for him, in which case he supplies an invoice and instructions, and the shipping company undertakes this business. A small charge is made for the extra work entailed.

The bills of lading are made out in 'sets', and any number may constitute the set according to the requirements of the particular trade. It is essential that at least one bill of lading be supplied, together with a copy bill of lading, known as the captain's copy, which is retained by the master for record purposes.

While the bill of lading is the document proper, the copy is of no value, and as many copy bills of lading may be included in the set as are desired either for the shipping company's purposes or for the shipper's own requirements.

The bills of lading, however, are of equal standing, and it is usual to find at the foot of the bill of lading the term — 'In witness whereof the

SHIPPER: No.

CARGO CONTROL NUMBER

VESSEL, VOYAGE, JOURNEY.   BILL NUMBER

Manchester Liners Ltd

ML

P.O. Box 189
Manchester Liners House
Port of Manchester
Manchester M5 2XA
Tel. 061-872 4466

Registered No.
57195 England

CONSIGNEE (IF ORDER, STATE NOTIFY PARTY)   No.

CUSTOMS No.	H/H	P/H	H/P	P/P

AGENT/FRT FWDR   No.

NOTIFY:-

PLACE OF ORIGIN	AGENTS REF.

INLAND TRANS/VESSEL

OCEAN VESSEL   PORT OF LOADING   SHIPPERS REF.

PORT OF DISCHARGE   * FINAL DESTINATION   JOB NUMBER   INLAND ROUTING

CONTAINER NUMBERS   TARE WEIGHT   NUMBER AND KIND OF PACKAGES, DESCRIPTION OF GOODS   CONTENTS   CONTENTS
SEAL NUMBERS   MARKS & NUMBERS   WEIGHT = Kg   MEASUREMENT = M^3

RATE OF EXCHANGE				FREIGHT PAYABLE	
DESCRIPTION	QUANTITY	RATE		INLAND AT	
			OCEAN AT		
			PREPAID	COLLECT	

FREIGHT PAYABLE / INLAND AT

"Received for loading/shipped in apparent good order and condition on board the vessel named herein, (after receipt at Inland Depot where applicable), the goods or packages or containers of merchandise stated to be marked, numbered and described herein (weight, measure, brand, contents, quality and value unknown) subject always to the Exceptions, Limitations, Conditions and Liberties as set out in the carriers Bill of Lading a copy of which is available in all Manchester Liners Ltd. offices and Agents offices at Shippers/Receivers request.

"In witness whereof, there have been executed .... Bills of Lading, all of this tenor and date which have been signed by the said Carrier, one of which being accomplished the others to stand void."

"In the case of a Waybill goods will be released to named Consignee without production of this document."

DATED IN

FOR THE OWNERS OF THE ABOVE NAMED SHIP

MANCHESTER LINERS LIMITED

Per .... BY AUTHORITY OF THE MASTER.

* APPLICABLE ONLY WHEN DOCUMENT USED
AS A THROUGH BILL OF LADING.

THE VESSELS AGENTS AT PORT OF DESTINATION ARE DESIRED TO NOTIFY THE ABOVE-MENTIONED THE ARRIVAL OF THE VESSEL, BUT IT IS AGREED THAT NO RESPONSIBILITY SHALL ATTACH TO THE VESSEL OR OWNERS OR AGENTS IF THERE SHOULD BE ANY FAILURE TO MAKE SUCH NOTIFICATION.

ZIPLOCK by Moore Paragon   MANCHESTER LINERS FORM REF. C14 (AMENDED 14/2/79)

master or agent hath affirmed . . . . bills of lading all of this tenor and date, the one of which being accomplished the others stand void.' The number of bills of lading which constitute the set are entered in the blank space.

The shipper usually affirms to three bills of lading, one for his own records, one for his consignee, and a second copy for the consignee sent usually by the following mail in case the first copy forwarded him is lost or delayed.

The master of the ship is instructed to deliver the goods to the person who produces a bill of lading, and therefore it is in the interest of all shippers, where more than one bill of lading is issued, to see that the consignee is the person who receives it. The master, in the absence of knowing that the holder of the bill of lading has no right to it, or in the absence of known fraud, has authority to deliver the goods. In the event of any goods being so delivered to another person who holds the document of title but is not authorized, the master is free from liability for wrongful delivery.

In describing bills of lading it must be remembered that nearly all bills of lading were originally 'received for shipment' bills of lading, which state that the goods have been received for shipment on board the vessel. Here, there is *no* actual receipt for goods which have been shipped.

The Carriage of Goods by Sea Act contains a stipulation that if a shipper so demands, he shall have issued to him a shipped bill of lading when the cargo is loaded. This commences 'shipped on board the vessel ...', and states that the goods are actually on board.

Bankers are reluctant to accept documents that do not clearly set out this important statement, and many demand 'shipped' bills of lading. Many shipping companies now only print shipped bills of lading.

As there is no implied or express demand for a seaworthy ship (see Carriage of Goods by Sea Act 1971), the term 'shipped on board the *good* ship' is rarely seen, it being 'shipped on board the vessel ...'.

The next clause for consideration is that of 'apparent good order and condition'. The full opening phrase on a bill of lading is 'Shipped (or received) in apparent good order and condition on board the vessel . . . .'. This phrase means that the outward condition of the goods on being received by the ship, is in good order; the shipowner in effect says: 'I can only judge by exterior proof as to the soundness of the goods received, and apparently they are in good order.' To earn his freight the carrier is only bound to carry the goods and deliver them in the same order in which he received them. If they were in apparent good order, on shipment, it is his duty to deliver them in like apparent good order and condition.

Should the goods have any defects, then the carrier will qualify the term 'apparent good order' by including in the margin of the bill such terms as 'old case', 'stained case', 'straw wrapped pieces only', or 'unprotected'. The addition of any similar qualifying clause makes the bill of lading 'unclean', and conversely, the expression 'clean bill of lading' means any bill of lading which has the clause 'apparent good order and condition' unqualified.

Shipping companies in their own interest insert these clauses when necessary as a safeguard against unwarranted claims.

There is a practice of issuing letters of indemnity against clean bills of lading, which is adopted by a number of companies. These letters of indemnity state that in consideration of being given a clean bill of lading the holder indemnifies the carrier against all risks and claims arising from the defect. This, although practised, is legally wrong, and the holder of a letter of indemnity in this case has no right other than that of good faith.

The master of the vessel having signed for so many cases in apparent good order and condition, when he knows they are not so by being given a letter of indemnity to that effect, issues a legal document in the form of the bill of lading with a misstatement of fact upon it, which is nothing less than a common fraud, and on these grounds numerous cases fail because the owners are unable to seek the assistance of the letter of indemnity.

The bill of lading is made out in the name of the shipper, or, if an agent, as 'A.B. as agents', and consigned to the consignee or receiver. For many reasons, such as confidentiality, some shippers are anxious that the name of the consignee shall not become known, and in this case the bill of lading is consigned to 'order' or 'shipper's order'.

When goods are consigned to a named consignee, the shipper has no need to endorse the bill of lading before forwarding to his consignee, but when it is consigned to 'order' he must endorse the bill over to the consignee to whom he wishes delivery made.

Other clauses appear in the body of the bill, but the clause paramount of the Carriage of Goods by Sea Act makes it unnecessary to deal with these here.

The bill is signed at the foot by, or for, the master. He, as the agent for the owners in the care of the vessel, and bailee for the cargo during the period of its shipment, is personally responsible for the goods while in his care. This matter is dealt with fully in chapter 11.

If a bill of lading is signed for goods which are not actually on board, the liability of the master is increased, for it may happen that the bill is issued, and therefore the *prima facie* evidence is that the goods were actually shipped, and the carrier may have great difficulty in proving that this was not so. It is conclusive to a holder for value.

It is therefore the master's duty, or the duty of any one having authority to sign for the master, to see that the particulars in the bill of lading are accurate, before the bill is issued.

The date which appears at the foot of the bill should of course be the actual date of shipment, or receipt of the goods. This traditional bill of lading is now known as the 'long form' bill of lading.

In the body of the bill the ports of shipment and delivery are mentioned, and the contract is therefore to carry the goods with all

BILL OF LADING

B/L No.

Shipper's Ref.

F/Agent's Ref.

BEN OCEAN

BEN LINE STEAMERS LIMITED
BLUE FUNNEL LINE LTD.
GLEN LINE LTD.
NEDERLANDSCHE STOOMVAART
MAATSCHAPPIJ "OCEAAN" BV

Managers: **Wm. Thomson & Co., Edinburgh**

Shipper		
Consignee (if "Order" state Notify Party)		
Notify Party (ONLY if not stated above: otherwise leave blank)		
*From (Local port of loading)		
*Local vessel	Port of loading	
Ocean vessel		
Port of discharge	*Final destination (if on-carriage)	
Marks and Numbers	Number and kind of packages; description of goods	Freight payable at

	Number of Bs/L signed	
	Gross Weight	Measurement

*Applicable only when document used as a Through B/L

ABOVE PARTICULARS DECLARED BY SHIPPER

SHIPPED in apparent good order and condition unless otherwise stated herein the goods described above either on board the above local vessel in or off the local port named above, or (if no local vessel is named above) on board the above ocean vessel, for carriage subject to the conditions set out overleaf to the port of discharge or destination (as the case may be) named above or so near thereto as the carrying vessel may safely get and delivery thereat to the consignee or his or their assigns. If any part of the carriage is performed otherwise than by a vessel operated by the Carrier such part of the carriage shall be subject to the provisions of Clause 10 overleaf.

In accepting this Bill of Lading the shipper, consignee and/or the owners of the goods, and the holder of this Bill of Lading, expressly accept and agree to all its stipulations, conditions and exceptions, whether written, printed, stamped or incorporated on the front or back hereof, as fully as if they were all signed by such shipper, consignee, owner or holder. This Bill of Lading shall be construed and governed by English Law, and shall apply from the time the goods are received for shipment until delivery, but always subject to the conditions and exceptions of the carrying conveyance; it shall be given up, duly endorsed, in exchange for delivery order if required.

FREIGHT PARTICULARS

IN WITNESS whereof the master or agent of the ocean vessel has signed the number of Bill of Lading stated above, all of this tenor and date, one of which being accomplished, the others shall stand void.

Number of Packages (in words)

_____

Dated at _____
For the Ship

Agents

(Continued on Reverse side)

CONDITIONS

IT IS MUTUALLY AGREED THAT:—

1. (a) If at the place of shipment on board the Carrier's vessel there is in force the Carriage of Goods by Sea Act, 1924 (hereinafter in this Clause called "the English Act") or any Statute, Ordinance or Law substantially in the same terms (save as to voyages to which it applies) as the English Act this Bill of Lading is to have effect subject to the Rules contained in the Schedule to the English Act or contained in or scheduled to such Statute, Ordinance or Law as applied thereby and the Carrier shall be entitled to all the privileges, rights and immunities contained in the English Act or such Statute, Ordinance or Law or Rules as if the same were specifically set out herein.

(b) If at the place of shipment on board the Carrier's vessel there is in force any Statute, Ordinance or Law (hereinafter in this sub-paragraph called "restrictive legislation") controlling or restricting the free right to contract for the carriage of goods by sea otherwise than as aforesaid, this Bill of Lading shall nevertheless be subject to the Rules (other than Article IX) contained in the Schedule to the English Act and the Carrier shall be entitled to the benefit of the provisions contained in Sections 2, 5 and 6 (2) of the English Act in the same manner as he would have been entitled if the English Act had applied to this Bill of Lading, provided always that to the extent to which any of the said Rules or of the said Sections of the English Act or any other terms, conditions or exceptions herein contained are inconsistent with or repugnant to any such restrictive legislation, then to that extent but no further, that Rules, Section, term, condition or exception, as the case may be, shall cease to have effect.

(c) If at the place of shipment on board the Carrier's vessel no such Statute, Ordinance or Law as is referred to in sub-paragraphs (a) or (b) hereof is in force, this Bill of Lading shall be subject to the Rules (other than Article IX) contained in the Schedule to the English Act and the Carrier shall be entitled to the benefit of the provisions contained in Sections 2, 5 and 6 (2) of the English Act in the same manner as he would have been entitled if the English Act had applied to this Bill of Lading.

Nothing herein contained shall be deemed to be a surrender by the Carrier of any of his rights or immunities or an increase of any of his responsibilities or liabilities under the said Rules, Statute, Ordinance or Law as so applied or incorporated.

Provided that (in the application of any of the foregoing provisions of this Clause) (a) if any Clause, covenant or agreement herein in part contravenes such Statute, Ordinance or Law or the said Rules as the case may be and in other part is capable of being construed so as not to contravene and is permissible under such Statute, Ordinance or Law or the said Rules as the case may be such last mentioned part shall be deemed to be included in the agreement between the Carrier and the Shipper and that (b) any agreement, stipulation, condition, reservation or exemption herein contained which is capable of application to the custody and care and handling of the goods prior to the commencement of loading on and subsequent to the completion of discharge from the Carrier's vessel shall be deemed to apply thereto notwithstanding that it may contravene the Law affecting any other part of the transit.

(d) Nothing in this Clause shall have the effect of imposing on the Carrier any obligation, either under such Statute, Ordinance, Law or Rules or otherwise whatsoever, otherwise than in respect of carriage on board a vessel operated by the Carrier.

2. **Exemptions and immunities of all servants and Agents of the Carrier**. It is hereby expressly agreed that no servant or Agent of the Carrier (including every independent contractor from time to time employed by the Carrier and every servant or agent of every such independent contractor) shall in any circumstances whatsoever be under any liability whatsoever to the Shipper, Consignee or Owner of the goods or to any Holder of this Bill of Lading for any loss, damage or delay of whatsoever kind arising or resulting directly or indirectly from any act, neglect or default on his part while acting in the course of or in connection with his employment and, but without prejudice to the generality of the foregoing provisions in this Clause, every exemption, limitation, condition and liberty herein contained and every right, exemption from liability, defence and immunity of whatsoever nature applicable to the Carrier or to which the Carrier is entitled hereunder shall also be available and shall extend to protect every such servant or Agent of the Carrier acting as aforesaid and for the purpose of all the foregoing provisions of this Clause the Carrier is or shall be deemed to be acting as Agent or trustee on behalf of and for the benefit of all persons who are or might be his servants or Agents from time to time (including independent contractors, their servants or agents as aforesaid) and all such persons shall to this extent be or be deemed to be parties to the contract in or evidenced by this Bill of Lading.

3. The Carrier shall not be responsible for any loss or deterioration of or damage or delay to the goods or any part thereof howsoever caused (whether by unseaworthiness or unfitness of the ship or of any other ship, tender, lighter, or craft, or any other mode of conveyance whatsoever or otherwise howsoever) during the periods which, in relation to the goods or that part thereof as the case may be, are prior to the commencement of the loading thereof on to the ship and after the completion of the discharge thereof from the ship. In the event of any inconsistency between the provisions of this Clause and of any other provisions contained in this Bill of Lading, the provisions of this Clause shall prevail.

4. **Route**. The Carrier does not contract to proceed by the shortest or by the geographical or customary or advertised route (if any) and the ship or other method of conveyance may for any purpose whatsoever whether connected with the joint adventure or not and whether before the beginning or at any time or stage of the voyage proceed by any course or route whatsoever although in a contrary direction to or out of or beyond the direct or geographical or customary or advertised route to the place of delivery once or oftener in any order backwards or forwards without notice to Shippers or Consignees and for any such purpose may call and/or remain or omit to call and/or remain at any port or ports, place or places whatsoever and may carry the goods back to the port of loading or to any port or place whether beyond the port of delivery or not and may make any delay whatsoever at or in sailing from the port of loading or any such port or place as aforesaid. The said goods or any part thereof may at the Carrier's option at any time or times during the transit whether before or after shipment be carried in a substituted ship or transhipped to any other ship or landed or stored or put into hulk or craft or lighter or reshipped on the same or any other ship or ships proceeding by any route or may be forwarded by lighter, rail or any other conveyance belonging to the Carrier or not and even though the said goods or any part thereof are detained or delayed in the course of such shipment, transhipment, landing, storage or reshipment.

For the purpose of this contract all such proceedings and calls and all such departures from the direct, geographical, customary or advertised route and all such delays, detentions, shipment, transhipment, landings, storages, reshipments and forwarding shall be included in the contract of carriage herein provided for and shall form part of the contractual voyage notwithstanding any reference to the place of shipment or delivery or any other provision whatsoever herein contained.

5. The ship shall have liberty to tow and assist vessels in all situations, to be towed, to sail with or without pilots, adjust compasses, to drydock with the goods on board, to carry cargo of all kinds dangerous or otherwise and to comply with orders given or purporting to be given by any Government, Harbour, Dock or Canal Authority. Anything done or not done in pursuance of this Clause shall be deemed to be within the contract of carriage herein provided for and to form part of the contractual voyage.

railway station within or nearest to destination and must be taken away by the Consignees immediately after arrival.

11. **Discharge and Delivery**. The goods may be discharged from the ship as soon as she is ready to unload and as fast as she is able continuously day and night, Sundays and holidays included, on to wharf or quay, or other spaces, open or covered or into store, hulk, lazaretto or lighters, whether insulated, bonded or not, at ship's option and at the risk and expense of the Owners of the goods, any custom of the port to the contrary notwithstanding, and always subject to the regulations and conditions of any such wharf or quay, spaces, store, hulk, lazaretto or lighters, whether the property of the Carrier or other persons, to which regulations and conditions the Owners of the goods hereby authorise the Carrier to agree on their behalf. If discharge is impeded by Consignees not taking delivery as fast as the ship can discharge, such Consignees shall pay the Carrier demurrage at the rate of [redacted] sterling per gross registered ton per day for any detention caused to the ship, and the goods may at Carrier's discretion be carried on and discharged at the first convenient port, which shall for all purposes be considered the port of discharge under this Bill of Lading.

12. **Notification**. Any clause hereon giving names of parties who desire to be notified of ship's arrival at destination is solely for the information of ship's. Agents and failure to notify shall not involve the Carrier in any responsibility or relieve the Consignees from any obligations hereunder.

13. **Master Porterage and Wharfingering**. Notwithstanding any custom of the port to the contrary, the Carrier, Master or Agents may appoint any firm or persons to receive, remove, sort, stack, watch, weigh, measure and deliver the goods on behalf of the Consignees, who shall pay to such firm or persons the current rate for all work performed on their behalf and indemnify the Carrier from all risks and expenses incurred.

Where, under any Statute or regulation at the port of discharge, goods carried hereunder are delivered to a Licensed Wharfinger as custodian or bailee thereof whether as Agent to the Carrier or otherwise, the Shipper, Consignee and/or Owner of the said goods shall not make against the Wharfinger aforesaid whether as custodian, bailee, Agent or otherwise any claim howsoever arising for an amount exceeding the declared value of goods paying freight on an *ad valorem* basis or the invoice value whichever shall be least or in the case of other goods, the invoice value or £100 per package or unit whichever shall be least and further the Shipper, Consignee and/or Owner aforesaid shall indemnify the Carrier against all or any liability whatsoever to the said Wharfinger arising by reason of any such claim having been made or satisfied including liability arising from any express indemnity in respect of such claims given by the Carrier to such Licensed Wharfinger.

14. Where **Customs** at port of transhipment or delivery require any bond or undertaking before permitting the landing or forwarding of dutiable goods the Carrier, Master or Agents are hereby authorised to give such undertaking on behalf of Owners of the goods who shall indemnify the Carrier from all risks and expenses incurred. The Carrier and/or Master Porter are authorised by the Owners of dutiable cargo at any port, during and after discharge, at their sole discretion, to incur and pay Customs charges for watching such cargo which charges the Owners thereof undertake to repay, any custom of the port to the contrary notwithstanding.

15. **Goods not permitted to be landed** at destination may be discharged at any other port or ports or returned to the port of loading by land or water, all at the risk and expense of the Owners of the goods, who shall pay freight for return carriage.

16. **A valuable package** is one of which the contents exceed in value twenty-five pounds sterling per cubic foot, if measurement cargo, or per half hundredweight, if weight cargo. The Shipper shall declare to the Carrier before shipment the nature and value of goods contained in all valuable packages shipped by him. Consignees must take delivery of valuable packages from on board during ship's stay in port, failing which they may be landed and stored or carried on at the risk and expense of the Owners thereof.

17. **Choice of Rates and Limits of Liability**. For the purpose of determining the rate of freight and the liability of the Carrier in respect of the goods hereby receipted for, it is mutually agreed that the value of such goods does not exceed £ 100 per package or unit and that in consideration of the rate of freight at which this shipment is accepted no greater value shall be placed on said goods in computing any liability whatsoever of the Carrier in respect thereof, as Carrier or otherwise, than the invoice value not exceeding such limitation, provided that if the Shipper in booking shipment of said goods has declared to the Carrier a greater value and freight in accordance with Carrier's valuable cargo tariff in excess of the ordinary tariff rate has been paid or agreed to be paid and the nature of the goods and such greater value are declared before shipment and inserted in this Bill of Lading, then in such case the liability of the Carrier in respect of said goods shall be computed on the basis of the invoice value not exceeding such greater declared value.

18. **Claims**. Any claims that may arise hereunder must be made at the port of delivery for determination and settlement at that port only. In no circumstances shall liability exceed the actual loss or damage sustained; the Carrier shall not be liable for any consequential or special damages and shall have the option of replacing any lost or damaged goods. Any sums paid to or recovered by Customs Authorities under any Bond for exportation given by the Shippers or Owners of goods shall not be considered to form part of any actual loss or damage sustained by or in connection with such goods for which the Carrier is or shall be liable.

If the ship comes into collision with another ship as a result of the negligence of the other ship and/or the negligence of any ship or ships other than or in addition to the colliding ship and any act, neglect or default of the Master, Mariners, Pilot or the servants of the Carrier in the navigation or in the management of the ship the Owners of the goods carried hereunder will indemnify the Carrier against all loss or liability to the non-carrying ship and/or any other ship or ships as aforesaid or her or their Owners in so far as such loss or liability represents loss of or damage to or any claim whatsoever of the Owners of the said goods paid or payable by the non-carrying ship and/or any other ship or ships as aforesaid or her or their Owners to the Owners of the said goods and set off, recouped or recovered by the non-carrying ship and/or any other ship or ships as aforesaid or her or their Owners as part of their claim against the carrying ship or Carrier

At any port where, in accordance with Customs regulations, the goods have to be landed into the charge of the Customs or other Authorities no claims for shortage or damage will be considered by the Carrier, beyond that noted by the Authorities at the time of receiving the goods into their charge.

19. **Apportionment**. Unidentifiable or surplus goods may be apportioned amongst claimants, if any, for short or incorrect delivery of like goods, who shall accept such apportionment to the extent thereof. The Carrier or his Agents may at their discretion sell unclaimed perishable goods forthwith and other unclaimed goods after three months from date of discharge, and payment to the Owners of the goods of the net proceeds of the sale less freight and charges, if any, shall free the Carrier from all liability.

20. Breakage of **Glass, China, Castings** and other goods of a brittle or fragile nature shall be taken to be due to inherent defect, quality or vice of the goods or insufficiency of packing in the absence of evidence of negligence, fault or failure in the duties and obligations of the Carrier.

reasonable speed from the one place to the other. A clause is found in many bills allowing the carrier the privilege of deviating to other ports 'in any order whatsoever, backwards or forwards in any directions'. This clause is valueless as there is no permission at any time for the owner to leave his course. Where this route is an advertised one, and the shipper is aware that by custom of trade the vessel calls at intermediate ports, e.g. London — South Africa, calling at Cape Town, Durban and Port Elizabeth, he accepts this route, but does not give the carrier permission to take his vessel to Liverpool after leaving London.

'Through' bills of lading are issued when a shipper wishes the carrying company to make arrangements for a complete journey, and these bills of lading in addition to the agreement to carry goods from port to port include a further journey (by sea or land) from the port of ship's destination to a distant place. In this case the carrier incorporates in the bill of lading a clause stating that the goods are to be 'transhipped and forwarded to . . . . . . at ship's expense but at shipper's risk.'

An additional charge is made for this extended journey, and the carrier bears all expenses of shipping and transhipping, but from the time the goods leave his care he repudiates all responsibility for their safe carriage. This extra journey is outside the contract of affreightment, and the terms and conditions of the bill of lading do not apply.

The carrying company is merely acting as agent in arranging the on-carriage.

Combined transport bill of lading. This is a comparatively recent development. It is a negotiable document (or can be) and the combined transport operator takes charge of the goods at a place of acceptance and provides an undertaking to deliver the goods at a designated place of delivery against surrender of the document. A clause in the document that the goods are to be delivered to the order of a named person, or to the bearer, constitutes the undertaking. The combined transport operator accepts full responsibility for the entire journey and acts as principal vis-à-vis the shipper and other carriers.

Since the repeal in 1949 of stamp duty on bills of lading, copy bills (i.e. bills other than the number of bills to the set) are stamped 'Copy Bill of Lading — not negotiable' or similar wording. In some cases different coloured bills are used to distinguish copies from negotiable bills.

For bills of lading under charter-parties, the above conditions apply with a few exceptions, the most important of which is that the conditions of a bill of lading are always subservient to the charter-party clauses. When a charter-party is issued, this is a contract pure and simple, and the bill issued under such document is only a receipt with all terms as per *charter-party*. The effect of the Carriage of Goods by Sea Act in this connection is dealt with fully in the next chapter.

The Bill of Lading Act 1855 is a small but valuable act, and its provisions are briefly:

(*a*) It gives the consignee or endorsee to whom the property passes, all rights of suit as if the contract had been made with him originally.

(*b*) It preserves the right of stoppage *in transitu*, the right to claim freight against the shipper, or any other liabilities of the consignee.

(*c*) It provides that the bill of lading in the hands of the consignee for valuable consideration is conclusive evidence of the shipment having been made, even though the goods were not shipped, unless the holder has been advised that the goods were never on board.

Considerable national and international thought has been given to the problem of simplifying the paper-work entailed in the production of the commercial documents relating to an export consignment. These are the various forms required by carriers, customs authorities, port authorities, forwarding agents, banks, and insurance companies. These efforts resulted in two documents, the 'common short form of bill of lading' and the 'sea waybill'.

The short form of bill of lading came from a more general rationalization in maritime transport documents as recommended by the United Nations. This short form was recognized by the International Chamber of Commerce in 1974. It was agreed that, unless specifically prohibited by the terms of an individual credit, 'short form' bills of lading could be used in credits issued in accordance with ICC's Uniform Customs and Practice for Documentary Credits. On 2 April 1979 the General Council of British Shipping (GCBS) and the Simplification of International Trade Procedures Board (SITPRO) took these developments a stage further and introduced the common short form of bill of lading, it being recommended by both organizations. This short form retains the legal protection afforded by the 'long form' bill of lading. Instead of conditions and clauses in small print, it has on the front a short incorporation clause which advises shipowners that details of the conditions of carriage are available separately. This clause has been agreed between the GCBS and underwriters and should be given equal effect under English law as if the conditions had been printed in full on the form. This common short form bill of lading is a 'received for carriage' document, which can be converted into a 'shipped' or 'loaded on board' document by notation of the carrier as stated in the Carriage of Goods by Sea Act.

The common short form of bill of lading is not only for shipowners who are members of GCBS but is available for outward liner shipments from the UK. By agreement it can be used instead of the shipowner's own form and act as a port-to-port or through bill of lading, for containerized, groupage or general cargo. A common short form of bill of lading is a document of title to the goods by endorsement and transfer, or the goods pledged or mortgaged as security for an advance. Like the 'long form', this does not give the transferee a better title than that held by the person making the transfer.

The sea waybill is a non-negotiable document. It came into being largely because of faster ships and the very swift turn-round particularly of container ships on the short sea routes between the UK and the

Continent and Scandinavia, which had lead to a situation where ordinary bills of lading were failing to arrive in time.

In January 1977 the GCBS and SITPRO introduced the common short form sea waybill. It provides a receipt for goods by the carrier and is evidence of the contract of carriage as described. It has the protection vis-à-vis its construction in English law with underwriters and it also possesses the incorporation clause regarding conditions of carriage similarly to the short form of bills of lading.

Care should however be exercised to ensure that the country of destination does not prevent the use of waybills. In a similar way to bills of lading, sea waybills can be converted into a 'shipped' or 'loaded on board' document by the carrier, and can then be transmitted through a bank for collection, but if a UK bank is required to advance finance on the strength of the document, a shipped bill of lading is normally required.

Both the common short form of bill of lading and the sea waybill contribute to economies in that carriers do not insist on their own forms and therefore the forms can be used for various lines and trades and also much time can be saved in preparing documents. This time factor is important in avoiding delayed documentation and should benefit commerce by being both quicker and cheaper.

6 Carriage of Goods by Sea Act 1971

The Carriage of Goods by Sea Act 1924, which introduced many changes in the laws of shipping, was the outcome of many conferences between shipowners and shippers.

It had been felt that for some years carriers, by the incorporation of so many clauses and exemptions, were obtaining an unfair advantage over shippers, who had little choice by lack of organized opposition than to accept the bill of lading adopted by the carrying company.

As a result of discussions between all interested parties, including bankers and insurance officials, an International Conference was held in Brussels during the year 1922–23 for the purpose of establishing liabilities, responsibilities, rights and immunities of carriers under bill of lading shipments.

Legislative effect was given to the rules formulated at the Conference by the 1924 Act, so far as the United Kingdom was concerned, while many other countries have passed similar statutes. The American Carriage of Goods Act, passed during 1936, was the last of these statutes. In the American Act, however, application is made to goods to or from American ports.

In 1968 a convention was held in Brussels, attended by ten nations, each of whom had not less than one million gross registered tons of shipping under their flag, and this meeting resulted in a protocol being signed unifying certain rules of law relating to bills of lading.

The Carriage of Goods by Sea Act 1971, incorporating the amendments in the protocol, was passed by Parliament in 1971, and a Commencing Order was signed by the Minister of State in June 1977, bringing the act into operation in the United Kingdom.

The provisions of the act are set out in the appendix at the end of this volume, and here the various provisions are dealt with individually.

Section 1. The introductory paragraph (1) reminds the reader that the act applies the amended Hague Rules, and (2) that the provisions of the rules shall have the force of law.

(3) The act states that it shall effect in relation to the carriage of goods by sea from a United Kingdom port.

(4) Directs attention to the fact that the act only applies to cases where a bill of lading or similar document is to be issued.

(5) Refers to the powers of the Secretary of State to vary the sums for

which a carrier or ship may be liable (see Article IV.5 (a) and (b)).

(6) The rules shall have the force of law in relation to any bill of lading if the contract provisions require it or if any non-negotiable receipt is involved.

(7) Refers to the situation applicable in the case of deck cargo or live animals.

Section 2. Describes part of the range of the act when an appropriate order is made.

Section 3. States that there shall be no absolute warranty by the carrier to provide a seaworthy ship. This may appear startling as it was always a stipulation before the 1924 Act was brought into force that the carrier supplied a seaworthy ship, hence the expression 'Good ship', which is no longer necessary on bills of lading. But refer to Article III of the act to see that the carrier's responsibilities are not diminished.

Section 4. Extends the application of the act to other territories by means of Orders in Council.

Section 5. Further extends the application of the rules from ports in British possessions etc.

Section 6. Defines the title of the act, and (2) extends it to Northern Ireland.

(3) (a) Repeals the 1924 Act and (b) certain references to that act in other acts.

(4) States that certain exemptions from liability in the Merchant Shipping Act 1894 (as modified in the 1958 Act) relate to limitation of liability.

(5) Covers transitional provisions which may be introduced in the order bringing the act into force.

Schedule: the Hague Rules as amended by the Brussels Protocol 1968

Article 1. This contains definitions.

Para. (*a*). 'Carrier' includes the owner or charterer who enters into a contract with the shipper.

Para. (*b*) states that the contract of carriage applies only to contracts of carriage covered by bills of lading or any similar documents of title in so far as it relates to the carriage of goods by sea, including any bill of lading or similar document of title issued under or pursuant to a charter-party from the moment at which such bill of lading or similar document of title regulates the relations between carrier and a holder of same.

Although the latter part of this paragraph may seem to imply that bills of lading under charter-parties are covered by the act, and may appear contradictory to the latter part of Article 5, the explanation of Article 5 will make this point clear that under an ordinary charter-party contract the Carriage of Goods by Sea Act 1971 does not apply.

Para. (*c*) defines 'goods' omitting live animals and deck cargo. Live animals are always a matter for the carrier to make mutual agreement with the shipper, and as will be seen, few of the provisions of this act would be applicable.

Cargo carried on deck is also by way of special agreement. When a carrier accepts cargo it is always understood that such cargo shall be carried under-deck, and if cargo is of the nature that it has to be shipped 'on deck' then this again calls for special agreement and different terms of shipment. Deck cargo unless carried in accordance with custom of trade is always accepted 'at shipper's risk'.

Para. (*d*) classifies the term 'ship' as any vessel used for the carriage of goods by sea. A Merchant Shipping Act definition of a ship is 'any vessel other than one propelled by oars'.

Para. (*e*) defines the period of carriage from the time when goods are loaded to the time when goods are discharged from the ship. This term 'from the time when goods *are loaded*' may be taken to mean 'up to loading', as Article 2 states the carrier shall be subject to the responsibilities and liabilities, and entitled to the rights and immunities of the act in the loading, handling, stowage, carriage, custody, care and discharge of the goods. It will, therefore, be seen that if the carrier is responsible for the loading, handling, and stowage, these three operations come before the time when goods *are loaded*, and it must be agreed that the carriage of goods covers all the operations set out in Article 2.

This paragraph (*e*) sets out that the shipowner or carrier is not liable for the care and custody of the goods prior to loading or after discharge, as will be seen in Article 2.

It will also be noted that this act applies to 'through bills of lading' only during the period of sea carriage, and not for any additional time before or afterwards.

Article 3. This sets out the responsibilities and liabilities of the carrier —

Para. 1. Before, and at the beginning of each voyage, the carrier shall be bound to exercise his due diligence to (*a*) make his ship seaworthy, (*b*) properly man, equip, and supply the ship, and (*c*) make all holds refrigerated and cool chambers, and other parts of the ship in which goods are carried, fit and safe for their reception, carriage and preservation.

Here are the conditions that have been imposed in place of the old provision of a seaworthy ship. They are more detailed and demand more care. The carrier himself must exercise due diligence and the failure to comply with this regulation lays upon him the onus of proving his due diligence, which is obviously great.

It will also be noticed that the manning and equipping of a ship are part of the conditions. No ship is ever seaworthy unless it is properly manned — with sufficient crew on board for its safe navigation and control, and also a ship without complete equipment is certainly lacking part of its essentials.

Sub-para (*c*) is a reasonable condition also; it has always been understood — now compulsory by statute — that the holds must be in good condition for the reception of cargo. Giving an example of this, a vessel carrying bones, cargoes which are thankfully few, is not in a fit condition for the reception of other cargo until the holds have been completely scoured out. Greater detail on this point is needless.

Another example of an unseaworthy ship, which however is outside the scope of the act, is a vessel carrying live stock with foot and mouth disease, not being considered seaworthy for the carriage of further livestock until such a time as the vessel has been completely fumigated and the infection removed.

Para. 2 again recites under the heading of responsibilities, the duties mentioned in Article 2, viz. 'The carrier shall properly and carefully load, handle, stow, carry, keep, and care for, and discharge the goods.'

Para. 3 states that the carrier after he has received the goods into his charge, shall on demand of the shipper issue a bill of lading stating leading marks, which must be legible until the end of the voyage, number of packages or pieces, or the quantity, and the apparent order and condition of the goods, providing that the carrier need not show any of the above particulars which he thinks inaccurate, or which he has been unable to check — hence the qualifying term 'quality and contents unknown', which is often found in the body of the bill.

Such a bill issued is *prima facie* evidence of the receipt of the goods by the carrier. (Para. 4.)

Para. 5 states that the shipper shall be deemed to have guaranteed these particulars, and he shall indemnify the carrier against any inaccuracies. By this, however, the carrier does not limit his responsibilities and liabilities to any person other than the shipper.

Article 1 (B) of the act, referred to on page 29, modifies this paragraph, however, in those cases where the statement of the weight of a bulk cargo in a bill of lading is given by a third party other than the carrier or the shipper, such as a railway company or colliery company, provided that it is noted on the bill of lading as such, and the accuracy shall not be deemed to have been guaranteed by the shipper.

In Para. 6 of Article 3, there is the provision that unless notice of loss or damage be given in writing to the carrier or his agent before or at the time of the removal of the goods, or if the loss be not apparent within three days, such removal shall be evidence (*prima facie*) that the carrier has delivered the goods in accordance with the bill of lading.

This is the first occasion on which any limit of time for a notice of claim has been mentioned. The application of this paragraph to transhipment, or through cargo, is rather indistinct, and whether the notice of claim is timed from final delivery or delivery from ship is a point for much discussion.

Such notice as mentioned need not be given when goods have been jointly surveyed at the time of delivery.

The carrier and ship, however, are discharged from all liability for loss or damage unless suit is brought within one year from date of delivery, or time when goods should have been delivered. This does not mean that the claim must be settled; so long as a claim has been made or action started within the year, settlement may be any time afterwards.

The term 'suit' includes the matter of arbitration, which again must be commenced within the period stated.

When there has been any known loss both parties must give each other full facilities for inspection and tallying the goods. This latter provision may be compared with the 'sue and labour' clause of marine insurance.

Para. 7 of Article 3 provides that after the goods are loaded the bill of lading, if the shipper demands, shall be a 'shipped' bill of lading, provided any document of title previously taken up shall be surrendered.

From this section it will be seen that a shipped bill need only be given on demand, after goods have *been loaded*, whilst in Para. 3 of Article 3, a bill of lading (other than a shipped bill of lading) must be given when the goods are in the carrier's charge, but not necessarily on board.

The latter part of this section states that the receipt previously taken up, with the addition of the steamer's name and date of shipment noted thereon, may constitute a shipped bill. This of course refers to the coastal trade where it is often customary to issue receipts in lieu of bills of lading.

In Para. 8 of Article 3 there is the provision that any clause relieving the carrier from his responsibilities provided in the act shall be null and void, thus excluding the possible addition of many clauses which would defeat the purpose of the act.

A benefit of insurance is deemed a clause relieving the carrier from liability.

Article 4. Here are the rights and immunities of the carrier:

Para. 1. The carrier shall not be responsible for loss arising from unseaworthiness unless caused by lack of due diligence or by the failure of the carrier to carry out the provisions of Para. 1 of Article 3.

When such loss occurs the burden of proving exercise of due diligence is on the carrier or person claiming exemption under this paragraph. Earlier it was the reverse, when the onus of proof was on the person making the claim.

Para. 2 states that neither the carrier nor the ship shall be responsible for loss or damage from:

(*a*) Act, neglect, default, of the master, mariner, pilot, or servants of the carrier in the navigation or management of the ship.

This includes all causes not covered by Article 2 and Article 3, Para. 1, and it should be remembered that the management of the ship includes shore staff as well as the personnel on board. A ship is often managed or mismanaged by those in charge on land.

(*b*) Fire, unless caused by the privity or fault of the carrier.

Fire is always an excepted peril of common and public carriers.

(*c*) Perils, dangers, and accidents of the sea or other navigable waters.

This covers the extraordinary action of wind and waves, which cause damage to a ship. A ship, however, must be built to withstand the ordinary action of these elements, and it must be some happening out of the ordinary, and peculiar to the sea, to be included under this heading.

(*d*) Act of God.

Any action that may cause damage which could not have been prevented had any amount of care and human forethought been used beforehand; something beyond human control.

(*e*) Act of war.

Includes wars of all nations irrespective of the nationality of ship.

(*f*) Act of public enemies.

Any act of persons acting outside the law, such as pirates, etc.

(*g*) Act or restraint of princes, rulers or people or seizure under legal process.

Any act which is enforceable by persons acting under the law, e.g. royal proclamation, or government orders.

(*h*) Quarantine restrictions.

Covering all restrictions made or imposed by a medical officer or medical authorities in connection with quarantine.

(*i*) Act or omission of the shipper or owner of goods or his agent.

Carrier cannot be held liable for any act which may be caused by the neglect or omission of the shipper or owner of goods.

(*j*) Strikes, lock-outs, or restraint of labour from whatsoever cause whether partial or general.

A partial stoppage of labour in London would, however, give no excuse for protection under this clause for a ship loading at Glasgow, unless directly affected.

(*k*) Riots and civil commotion.

(*l*) Saving or attempting to save live or property at sea.

See notes under Para. 4 of this article.

(*m*) Wastage or loss from inherent defect or vice of the goods.

Inherent vice may be described as the natural tendency of goods to waste or become damaged, a common form of which is black rot in apples, causing considerable loss to many cargoes of apples over which the carrier has no control.

(*n*) Insufficiency of packing ⎱ responsibilities of
(*o*) Insufficiency of marks ⎰ the shipper.

(*p*) Latent defects not discovered by due diligence.

A latent defect may be described as an interior weakness which is not discoverable by exterior examination, such as a water pipe, faulty in its manufacture, but not discernible by ordinary examination.

(*q*) Any other cause arising without the actual fault or privity of a carrier or his agent.

Here again the burden of proof is upon the person who claims exemption through this section.

Para. 3 stipulates that the shipper shall not be responsible for any loss sustained by the carrier arising from any cause without the act, fault or neglect of the shipper, his agents or servants.

Para. 4 deals with one of the most important points of shipping law, which is deviation. It states that 'any deviation in saving or attempting to save life or property or any reasonable deviation shall not be deemed an infringement of the Rules, and the carrier shall not be liable for loss or damage resulting therefrom.'

Deviation may be divided into three types, deviation, justifiable deviation, and reasonable deviation. The term deviation means any departure from the set course of the voyage, and from the moment a vessel leaves her course the carrier loses all rights to the exemptions and immunities expressed in his bill of lading. But deviation may be made justifiable in cases where it is in the interest of all the parties, such as putting into a port of refuge, or deviating to save life or property. It is important to note that in this section the term life *or* property is stated. This is the second time (the first was in the 1924 Act) that any permission to save property alone has been incorporated in statute law or allowed in shipping. An explanation of the word 'reasonable', which is a word also found in this section, may be made by classing deviations of this type as deviations made in the interest of all parties concerned. Deviation in itself is something to be abhorred, for unless the master can secure a satisfactory decision, great loss and inconvenience may be caused to his owners. In extending the earlier remark, that from the time of deviation all exemptions and immunities are lost to the carrier, it is as well to point out that these are immediately lost, and they are not recoverable for the remainder of the trip, and the owner may suffer a loss perhaps two or three days after deviation occurred, and the vessel returned to her original course. It is, therefore, not advisable to accept this clause upon its face value.

Para. 5 (*a*) Amends the sum of maximum liability of 10,000 francs per packages or unit, or 30 francs per kilo of gross weight unless a higher value has been declared by shippers before shipment and inserted in the bill of lading. A definition of 'franc' is given in (*d*) of this section. (The 'franc' concerned is the French Poincaré gold franc.)

(*b*) Sets forth the method of assessing values recoverable.

(*c*) Covers the situation where goods are packed in a container or on pallets etc., or otherwise consolidated. But unless details of the number of packages or units are specified in the bill of lading as packed in such article of transport, then the article shall be considered the package or unit.

(*d*) Describes exactly how the value of the 'franc' shall be assessed.

(*e*) States that neither carrier nor the ship shall be entitled to the benefits of limitation of liability if it be proved that damage has resulted from wilful act or omission or recklessly with knowledge that damage would probably result.

(*f*) The declaration in (*a*) above, if contained in the bill of lading, shall be *prima facie* evidence, but not binding or conclusive on the carrier.

(*g*) The carrier and shipper may agree other maximum amounts than those specified in (*a*) above provided that no maximum amount so agreed is less than the appropriate maximum mentioned in (*a*).

(*b*) Neither shall the carrier or ship be responsible for any loss or damage where the nature or value has been knowingly mis-described.

Para. 6 refers to dangerous cargoes and states that when goods of an inflammable, explosive, or dangerous nature have been shipped without the knowledge of the master, they may be discharged or landed at any time or rendered innocuous, without compensation, and the shipper shall be liable for all damage or expenses arising out of such shipments. Also, when any such goods shipped with carrier's knowledge and consent become a danger to the ship they also may be treated in a similar manner without liability of the carrier, except to general average, if any. This freedom of action, without responsibility, is necessary for the master, and the decision to discard such cargo may be made in the interest of the ship, without the fear of heavy claims arising. This is one of the few occasions when the master is a free agent in respect of the treatment of the cargo.

Article 4 bis. Has four paragraphs all dealing with the conditions regarding the defences and limits of liability in any action against the carrier for loss or damage to goods covered by a contract of carriage. In the event of an action being brought against a servant or agent of the carrier, such servant or agent may avail himself of the defences and limits of liability which would apply to the carrier, but the total of amount recoverable shall not exceed the limits provided for in these rules. A servant or agents shall not be entitled to such protection if it be proved that the damage or loss resulted from action or omission wilfully or recklessly done with the knowledge that damage might or probably would result.

Article 5. This article sets out the conditions of any surrender of rights and immunities, and increase of responsibilities and liabilities.

The carrier may surrender all or part of his rights and immunities or increase his liabilities, provided such surrender or increase is incorporated in the bill of lading. There is no permission, however, for his rights and immunities to be increased and his liabilities to be surrendered. Clauses of this nature are prohibited by Para. 8 of Article 3.

The provisions of these rules are not applicable to charter-parties, but if bills of lading are issued, in the case of a charter-party, they must comply with the terms of the rules.

This provision may appear rather confusing, but it only covers cases similar to a ship being chartered and then placed on the loading berth to receive cargo. Many cases of this nature are found when companies running regular lines, by the damage or loss of a ship, find they must charter a vessel to continue their service and then under the period of the charter-party run the vessel on their regular route. It will be seen that the charter-party between the owner and charterer is outside the scope of the act, but the bill of lading contract between the charterer and his shippers comes under the regulations of the act, by reason of the fact that the terms and conditions of the bill of lading govern the contract of affreightment.

Where, however, a bill of lading is issued under a charter party, and is subsequently negotiated to a third or fourth party, from the time of the negotiation, the act applies to the bill of lading.

The final clause of Article 5 states that nothing in the rules shall prevent the insertion of any lawful provision regarding general average in the bills of lading.

Article 6. Notwithstanding the previous articles, carrier, master, or his agent, and a shipper may, in respect of particular goods, be at liberty to enter into any agreement in any terms as to responsibilities and liabilities, and rights and immunities or obligations as to seaworthiness, provided it is not contrary to the public policy, and provided no bill of lading has been issued and the terms shall be embodied in a non-negotiable receipt, which shall be marked as such. Provided that this article shall not apply to ordinary commercial shipments, but only to other shipments when the character or condition of the property is such as reasonably to justify a special agreement.

The meaning of the term 'particular goods' is still rather indefinite, but may be described as goods to which the application of the act would be impossible.

Article 7. There is nothing in the act to prevent a carrier or a shipper from entering into any agreement as to responsibility or liability of the carrier for goods prior to the loading on or subsequent to the discharging from ship. From this it will be seen that when 'through' bills of lading are issued, the act has no application to sections of the carriage of goods outside the actual carriage by sea.

Article 8. States that the rights and obligations of the carrier under any statute for the time being relating to limitation of liability of owners shall not be affected. This refers to the shipowners' liability, which is dealt with in chapter 4.

Article 9. States that these rules shall not affect the provisions of any international convention or national law regarding liability for nuclear damage.

Article 10. Itemizes the application of the rules to every bill of lading for the carriage of goods between ports in two different states and may be compared with the clause paramount in the 1924 Act if:

(*a*) the bill of lading is issued in a contracting state or,

(*b*) the carriage is from a port in a contracting state or,

(*c*) the contract contained in or evidenced by the bill of lading provides that these rules or legislation of any state given effect to them are to govern the contract, whatever may be the nationality of the ship, the carrier, the shipper, the consignee, or any other interested person.

Note: Should a bill of lading with reference to the 1924 Act be used, and a suit arise from some cause or action such bill of lading would be construed as if the 1971 Act were applied since it is superseding legislation.

7 Chartering and Charter-Parties

A chartering broker may be described as an intermediary between the shipowner and the merchant or the cargo owner. His knowledge must be extensive in order that he may cope with all requirements of his business; he must have a sound knowledge of shipping law, geography, port information, charges throughout the world, facilities at different places, distances between ports, and countless other matters. It also stands to reason that he must be of the highest character.

He acts between a shipowner who has tonnage idle, and a cargo owner who has a cargo which he wishes to be transported. He engages space for cargo and arranges the whole of the business details between the principals, receiving for his services the commission agreed under such arrangement.

When he fixes a contract of this nature it is known as a charter-party, of which there are three classes: *voyage, time,* and *demise.* The charter-party is a contract of affreightment, and for voyage charters is an agreement for the carriage of goods from one specific port to another, the owner of the vessel receiving freight for the cargo carried. In the case of time and demise charters, both of these contain a contract whereby the vessel is actually hired for a specific period of time, during which period the charterer has the freedom, within the stipulations of the charter-party conditions, of using the vessel for what purposes he may wish. In a demise charter the ownership to all intents and purposes changes hands for the period of the contract. The payment in this case is for the hire of the vessel, and an agreed amount is paid per month or per day for the use of the vessel.

In recent years a different form of demise charter has been developed to cater mainly for situations which arise usually from one of two causes. In one case, when governments hire or requisition ships (with or without crews) — as in time of war — to perform tasks which can contain elements of risk, and therefore the wording includes provision to cover perhaps extensive repairs beyond normal maintenance and possible terms of compensation in case of loss. The other case is when a new vessel is chartered as a part of or adjunct to a ship-building contract and from the moment of trials, owners in fact do not operate the vessel, but charterers do. This latter arrangement can sometimes last for the working lifetime of a ship. For instance, a tanker, specifically built to an oil company's requirements, and hired by them for say 20 years, but the construction not being financed by the oil company but by the owners. Such charters are referred to as 'bareboat charters'.

While in the case of bill of lading or liner shipments standard rates are charged, usually as agreed by the conference under which the vessel is operating, the rates for chartered ships fluctuate according to the state of the market, it being the tendency for rates to be high during busy periods, when tonnage is scarce, and low in slack times when idle ships are plentiful.

The arrangement of a charter-party is known as 'fixing' a charter, and when completed the vessel is termed 'fixed'. Brokers on the Baltic Exchange operate in a similar manner to those of the Stock Exchange.

Brokers are constantly in touch with the world's markets through the medium of the Baltic Exchange and can keep their principals – perhaps shipowners, perhaps merchants – advised of the daily trend of the markets and whether conditions tend towards rises or falls in rates, which fluctuations operate on the law of supply and demand as seen from the last paragraph.

Market reports are given in various shipping papers and a broker or owner who wishes to know the approximate state of a market with which he is not conversant can get a helpful lead from the fixtures reported. For instance the following may be reported:

US Gulf/Egypt – 25,000 t H. Grain, Sorghum, Soya Beans $39.85 F.I.O. 4 days/1,000 t 25 Sept. cancelling. (Fixed recently)

The explanation of this 'contraction would be:

A fixture on charter has been done for a cargo from a USA Gulf port to Egypt. The cargo to consist of 25,000 tonnes of heavy grain with options of loading sorghum and/or soya beans. The rate being agreed at $39.85 per tonne with 4 days allowed for loading and 1,000 tonnes per day for discharge. The cost of loading and discharge to be borne by the charterers. The vessel has to be ready to load not later than 25 September 1980. (This fixture was not reported at the time the fixture was made, hence the 'Fixed recently' explanation.)

A further fixture was reported:

Panjang/Bordeaux – Amsterdam range. 15,000 t Tapioca Products (Stowing 55 ft) $35.50 F.I.O. 21 days. Sept. 20–25.

The full details would read:

A fixture has been agreed to load a cargo from Panjang to one of a range of (suitable) ports chosen from those from and including Bordeaux to Amsterdam. The cargo consists of 15,000 tonnes of tapioca products stowing at not more than 55 cu.ft. per tonne at a rate of $35.50 on free in and out terms. A total of 21 days are allowed for loading and discharge, with laydays not before 20 September 1980 cancelling (if not ready to load) by 25 September 1980.

If, for example, an owner informs his broker that he has a ship expected ready at Benisaf on 30 December and asks what business can be obtained from Benisaf to a UK port, the broker will have a rough idea of the current rate ruling. He will certainly not let his owner fix his ship, for example, from Benisaf to Workington at £2.45 when the last rate was £2.49, unless of course, the market has suddenly fallen away.

Before proceeding to describe the contents of a charter-party and the meaning of clauses, there are several types of 'days' which are mentioned in chartering, and definitions of these are:

Lay days

Days agreed for loading and discharge. They may be separated into days for loading and days for discharge, or if agreed a total taken for the two operations, when days are then known as reversible-lay days. This is the time allowed under the charter-party, and a note of the agreed number of days will be shown in the charter-party.

Weather working days

Days for loading and discharge when the weather permits. Where weather working days are allowed, and work is commenced, time ceases to count if the work is held up owing to bad weather, or if weather makes the possibility of a start impracticable for the day. This applies only when work would otherwise be carried on.

Running days

Consecutive days, counting all days — Saturdays, Sundays, Bank Holidays, etc., the same.

Working days

In England a day of eight hours constitutes a working day, therefore a 24 hour day would be considered as three working days (if work is continuous), but in foreign countries this would alter according to the number of hours which constitute a working day in such places.

'Days'

It cannot be strongly enough emphasized that many troubles arise through careless wording of what is meant by 'days' in a charter-party. It must be specified exactly how they are to count.

Terminology

Charter-parties are known under different titles, some serving the purpose of a particular trade. In many cases a short title or code name is allotted for quick and short references. Here are a few examples of well-known charter-parties.

CHARTER PARTY FORMS

BAREBOAT	The Baltic and International Conference Standard Bareboat Charter	'BARECON "A" '
CEMENT	Chamber of Shipping Cement Charter Party 1922	'CEMENCO'
COAL (Including Coke and Patent Fuel)	Welsh Coal Charter Party 1896, To Danube, Rosario, R. Parana and Uruguay	No Code Name
	Chamber of Shipping East Coast Coal Charter Party, 1922. East Coast (Humber, Berwick) to Danube and River Plate	'MEDICON'
	Chamber of Shipping Coasting Coal Charter Party, 1913. Bristol Channel—Elbe/Brest and the United Kingdom	'WELCON'
	The Baltic and White Sea Conference Coal Charter Party, 1921. To Baltic, Scandinavia and White Sea	'BALTCON'
	The Baltic and White Sea Conference Polish Coal Charter, 1950	'POLCON'
FERTILIZERS	Chamber of Shipping Fertilisers Charter, 1942	'FERTICON'
GAS	Gas Voyage Charter Party to be used for Liquid Gas except LNG	'GASVOY'
GENERAL	The Baltic and International Maritime Conference Uniform General Charter (as revised 1922 and 1976)	'GENCON'
GRAIN	River Plate Charter Party, 1914, Homewards, River Plate and South America Homewards . .	'CENTROCON'
	Chamber of Shipping Australian Grain Charter, 1928	'AUSTRAL'
	Australian Grain Charter, 1972 . .	'AUSTWHEAT'
	North American Grain Charterparty 1973, issued by the Association of Ship Brokers and Agents (USA) Inc.	'NORGRAIN'
	Grain Voyage Charter Party, 1966 (Revised and Recommended 1974)	'GRAINVOY'

NITRATE	Hydrocharter Voyage Charter Party (Amended 1975)	'HYDRO-CHARTER'
ORE	Iron Ore Charter Party from Lower Buchanan, Liberia, to all Destinations	'LAMCON'
	The Baltic and International Maritime Conference General Ore Charter Party, 1962	'GENORECON'
	Soviet Ore Charter Party for Ores and Ore Concentrates from USSR Ports	'SOVORECON'
	The Japan Shipping Exchange Inc., Iron Ore Charter Party	'NIPPONORE'
STONE	Chamber of Shipping Stone Charter Party, 1920	'PANSTONE'
TANK	International Association of Independent Tanker Owners Tanker Voyage Charter Party 1976	'INTERTANK-VOY 76'
TIME	The Baltic and International Maritime Conference Uniform Time Charter (Traditional Layout) .	'BALTIME 1939'
	The Baltic and International Maritime Conference Uniform Time Charter Party for Offshore Service Vessels	'SUPPLYTIME'
WOOD (Including Pitwood, Props, Pulpwood, Roundwood and Logs)	Chamber of Shipping Baltic Wood Charter Party 1973	'NUBALTWOOD'
	Soviet Wood Charter Party 1961 .	'SOVIETWOOD'
	Black Sea Timber Charter Party for Timber from USSR Romanian Black Sea and Danube Ports . .	'BLACKSEA-WOOD'
	The Japan Shipping Exchange Inc., Charter Party for Logs 1967	'NANVOZAI'

Before fixing a charter-party the essential details that are required to be known are:

The draught of a vessel . . . . .   depth of water required to float a vessel. It must be remembered that to fix a ship with a depth of 23 ft. for a port where the maximum

	draught is 21 ft. would be useless, and the vessel would be unable to enter the port.
Size of holds	in order to be sure of the space available for cargo.
Particulars of derricks	on the ship. Their position and individual lifting capacity.

Bunker capacity.
Fuel consumption.
Rate of loading and discharge
and approximate weight to
measurement of cargo.
Loading and discharging ports.
Date of readiness.

The clauses necessary for every charter-party are named in the under-mentioned list and followed by explanations.

List of clauses

For all charter-parties the following clauses are essential, alternative clauses for time charters being shown.

(1) Title of the contracting parties.

(2) Name of the vessel.

(3) Warranty of seaworthiness of the vessel and the evidence.

(4) Description of the vessel.

(5) The loading and discharging ports. (For a time charter: the date of delivery and date of redelivery of vessel.)

(6) Cargo to be carried. (Time charters: the radius of trading.)

(7) Position of the vessel. (Time charters: date vessel will be ready and where.)

(8) Remuneration. (Voyage charters: freight. Time charters: hire.)

(9) Lay days and how they count. (Voyage charters only.)

(10) Days of demurrage and dispatch and the rate. (Voyage charters only.)

(11) Brokerage clause.

(12) Lien clause.

(13) Act of God clause.

(14) Exemptions from liability clause.

(15) Average clause.

(16) Arbitration clause.

(17) Penalty for non-fulfilment clause.

(18) Sub-letting clause.

(19) Deviation and salvage clause.

In addition to these the following may be found *only* in time charter-parties:

(1) Clause as to who pays fuel and port charges.

(2) Provision that time ceases on breakdown.

(3) Return of overpaid hire if vessel is lost.

(4) Charterer's right to complain of master and chief engineer.

(5) Charterer's obligation to provide master with full sailing directions.

(6) Bunkers on board.

(7) Drydocking.

(8) Bills of lading.

Voyage charters may also contain clauses in relation to the following matters:

(1) Limitation of liability clause (Cesser clause).

(2) Description of cargo.

(3) Options of other ports and cargoes.

Explanations of clauses

The explanations in brief of the foregoing clauses are:

(1) *Title of contracting parties.* Names of the charterer and owner of the ship.

(2) and (3) *Name of the vessel and warranty of seaworthiness, etc.* The warranty of seaworthiness may be in the form of the words 'good ship' with the class of the vessel added, e.g. good ship called the . . . . classed 100 A1 at Lloyd's.

It is well to remember that once a vessel has commenced loading the charterer cannot demand cancellation for unseaworthiness. Also, that although a ship may be 100 A1 at the commencement of the voyage, there is no obligation on the owners to keep this class during the period of the charter-party.

If a vessel is seaworthy for the voyage in prospect this is all that is necessary. In explanation of this point a vessel proceeding from *A* to *C via B*, has only to be seaworthy to reach *B* from *A*, and the owner must then make his vessel fit for the remainder of the voyage from *B* to *C* before the ship leaves port *B*.

(4) *Description of the vessel.* This is only contained in the gross and net tonnage of the vessel.

(5) *Loading and discharging ports.* This requires no explanation.

For a time charter-party this would not apply, as with a vessel being hired for a stated period there is no necessity or desire for the owner to know where the vessel is to load, and instead the time charter contains date of delivery of ship and date or redelivery, these being the two dates between which the charterer hires the vessel.

(6) *Cargo to be carried.* In a voyage charter this is stipulated together with the amount of cargo to be carried. This, again, is not necessary in a time charter, with the exception of the term 'any lawful merchandise' but the radius of trading is inserted. Radius of trading is usually very broad,

and a term similar to 'World-wide radius, ice-bound ports excepted' may be the only reference to this point.

(7) *Position of the vessel.* For voyage charters. A statement which must be perfectly correct in detail. If the owner states that the ship is 'now at Antwerp', and it is proved later that the vessel was not at Antwerp, charterers may claim cancellation of the charter-party. In a time charter the date when the vessel will be ready and place of delivery is given in place of the above clause.

(8) *Remuneration.* For voyage charter-parties freight is paid on the amount carried, but for time charters the payment is by hire for the period of the engagement.

(9) *Lay days and how they count.* This clause applies only to voyage charter-parties, as an owner is not concerned with the time that a vessel on time charter spends in loading and discharge.

(10) *Days of demurrage and dispatch and the rate.* The preceding explanation also applies to this clause. Should a vessel load and/or discharge in less than the prescribed time, owners of a ship pay dispatch money as a 'reward' for time saved. If, on the other hand, the time allowed is exceeded, then demurrage is payable at an agreed rate to the owner as 'compensation' for lost time.

(11) *Brokerage clause.* States the rate of brokerage that shall be paid.

(12) *Lien clause.* Giving owners of the vessel a right to hold cargo against payment of freight, or hire.

(13) *Act of God clause.* This is identical with the clause to be found in the Carriage of Goods by Sea Act, and has the same application.

(14) *Exemptions from liability clause.* This clause includes many occurrences from which owners claim exemption, and as the Carriage of Goods by Sea Act does not apply, there is no restriction. A few of these exemptions are:

(i) *Barratry.* Any wilful wrongdoing of the master and/or the crew without the connivance of the owners. Actions of the master or crew without the intention to defraud owners, or actions which cannot be described as criminal, are not included under this heading.

(ii) *Capture and seizure.* Acts of taking the ship by an enemy or belligerent, or the forcible taking of the ship.

(iii) *Queen's enemies.* Opposition forces of the Crown. The ship's nationality is its flag, and this clause may be read as any enemy of the country of the ship's nationality.

(iv) *Restraint of princes.* Every case where the voyage is interrupted by the supreme power of the country, such as an embargo, or prohibition of cargo.

(v) *Perils of the sea.* As described previously in the Carriage of Goods by Sea Act.

(15) *Average clause.* This clause states that general average, if any, shall be payable according to York-Antwerp Rules. As there are three sets of rules, the 1924, 1950 and 1974, the date must follow. The rules issued

later did not cancel the earlier codes, although the 1950 or 1974 rules are generally adopted.

(16) *Arbitration clause*. This sets out that any disputes shall be referred to arbitrators, and gives the conditions under which arbitration shall be carried out.

(17) *Penalty for non-fulfilment clause*. Gives the amount to be paid for default in carrying out the charter-party agreement.

(18) *Sub-letting clause*. This clause gives or refuses to allow permission for the vessel to be sub-let, or sub-chartered under the charter-party.

(19) *Deviation and salvage clause*. Allows or refuses to allow ship to deviate in order to save life or property, and also for the purpose of salvage.

The time charter-party clauses usually incorporated are as follows:

(1) *Clause as to who pays fuel and port charges*. This clause stipulates that all charges including the above are to be paid by the charterer.

(2) *Provision that time ceases on breakdown*. Commonly known as the *breakdown clause* — is inserted to adjust the hire when by reason of a breakdown the vessel ceases to operate. If by breakdown of machinery the vessel ceases to operate, the charterer is entitled to some return for lost time. The stipulation is usual for a period in excess of twenty-four hours, after which time ceases to count, and the charterer is credited with such time lost by the breakdown in his settlement for hire of the vessel.

(3) *Return of overpaid hire if vessel is lost*. Essentially a time-charter clause, stating that, should the vessel be lost, hire shall cease to be chargeable, and any amount overpaid shall be returned.

(4) *Charterer's right to complain of master and chief engineer*. This clause gives the right to the charterer of making any complaint to owners regarding these officers. They are left on board the ship by the owners, as their representatives, and also to be in 'possession' should owners wish to exercise a lien for hire money not paid. The charterer, not being the actual employer of these persons, must be given some power of authority, and such power is contained in this clause.

Some time charter-parties are fixed allowing the charterer to appoint the whole of the ship's personnel, including master and chief engineer. When this is the case, the charter is known as a *demise charter*, and is for all practical purposes a transfer of ownership of the vessel for the period of the charter, the owner having no control whatsoever over his vessel from the time she is hired until she is returned. This type of charter is often also known as a 'bareboat' charter.

(5) *Charterer's obligation to provide master with full sailing directions*. The master, in order to carry out instructions, must have full directions, and failure on the part of the charterer to supply these may entail delay and lost time.

The third list of clauses which are clauses a voyage charter may contain are:

(1) *Limitation of liability clause*. Known widely as the *cesser clause*,

and stipulates that 'Charterers' liability shall cease on the loading of cargo, and qualified payment of freight, dead freight, and demurrage.' When the charterer has loaded the cargo, and paid the charges incurred, his liability ceases.

(2) *Description of cargo.* This is phrased as 'The charterer shall load a full and complete cargo of . . . . not exceeding . . . . tons, not less than . . . . tons.' A full and complete cargo may be described as a quantity sufficient to sink the vessel to her load line in excess of tackle, provisions, furniture, etc. The two quantities are stipulations between which any amount constitutes a full and complete cargo.

(3) *Options of other ports and cargoes.* Gives permission for the vessel to carry other cargo than that fixed in the charter-party, usually, however, at the same rate of freight, and also the option of calling at other ports for loading and discharge.

The principal disputes which arise in connection with charter-party agreements are usually with reference to the meaning of clauses, and the ambiguous way in which they are drawn up, giving lack of definite expression. Protection and Indemnity Clubs to which reference will be made later, are always anxious that owners shall wherever possible fix ships upon some recognized charter-party form, in order to avoid possible extra liability.

The fact that charter-parties are generally printed does not prevent a charter-party being fixed on any other form. Charters may be made upon plain paper, by letter, or even by telegram, and it has been known for a charter-party to be drawn up on the back of an envelope.

By the adoption of a printed form, however, the conditions as printed may be altered or amended to suit the circumstances of charterer or owner, in which case alterations are made to the existing print. In these cases the written clauses and amendments always overrule the printed conditions; such alterations must, however, be made with care, as the alteration of one clause may lead to alteration through contradiction of many others.

Charter-parties may be made by word of mouth. Such a practice, however, is most unsatisfactory, as there is no proof of terms and conditions and this may prove to be disastrous. Charter-parties made by word of mouth of course are not stamped, there being no document to execute.

Several points raised in connection with charter-parties are given below:

Always afloat. Meaning that the vessel shall remain afloat during the whole of her loading or discharge, and shall at no time rest upon the bottom of the river or dock.

'Redelivered in like good order and condition.' Charterer must redeliver the ship after the period of the time charter has elapsed in the same condition as when he accepted her, with the proviso 'fair wear and tear excepted'. In some time charters the charterer has the right to paint the

funnel any colour he may wish – in order to make the ship uniform with his other vessels, if running on a regular service – but on redelivery of the ship, it is his obligation to repaint the ship's funnel its original colour. All damages must be repaired if they occur whilst under charter.

Brokerage. The broker is entitled to a commission for the business transacted under the charter-party, and this constitutes part of the contract. As, however, he is not a principal in the agreement, he is not entitled to sue for his commission, but may claim the protection of the charterer, and the principal is then bound to sue for the commission claimed. This in effect is the borrowing by the broker of the principal's name in order to overcome the point of law in this connection.

Representation or misrepresentation. Occasions arise where incorrect particulars are given in the charter-party, and any claims which may arise are judged upon the extent of such representation and its effect on the contract.

Signing charter-parties. If the charter-party is signed in an unqualified manner, then the signatories to it are considered the principals; therefore when a broker signs a charter-party for his principals he must qualify his signature accordingly. Should it be mentioned in the charter-party that 'John Brown' is acting as agent and reference be made to him as the agent, there is no necessity to state that he is the agent, as the charter-party is judged as a whole, but the agent should make this point clear by signing 'John Brown as Agent for the charterers', and where the contract has been fixed by telegraph, then he should make arrangements that his signature is qualified by the words, 'By Telegraphic Authority'.

Cases may occur where brokers are advised to fix a vessel of 800 tons, and upon confirmation being given discover that the tonnage should have been 8000. Unless they have agreed that contract by 'Telegraphic Authority', or some similar qualification, there is no recourse, and the charter must either be carried out, or cancelled; in either case a loss would probably be incurred.

Custom of trade. Custom of trade must be such that it is a recognized custom, and known generally by all engaged in that trade. Where this is pleaded or mentioned it overrules charter clauses, unless specifically excluded.

In voyage charter-parties it is recognized that notice of readiness or advice to the charterer that the vessel is ready to load in accordance with the terms of the agreement shall be given. This notice must be given before the lay days start to count, and may not be given until the ship is actually ready in all respects. This means that the ship must be ready to receive the cargo, and failure to have all holds ready – even though only one or two may be worked – for the reception of cargo makes the vessel unready. In the case of grain charter-parties, shifting boards or alternatives, which are to prevent the grain moving on voyage (see page 110, *post*), must be provided and be ready for use at the same time as the vessel, to claim perfect readiness.

A sailing telegram is sent when the vessel leaves for her port of loading, to acquaint the charterer of the position, in order that he may ascertain the date when the vessel will be an arrived ship and ready to be worked.

The charterer must arrange to supply his cargo when the ship is ready to load, and any delay is for his account; when his lay days are used, demurrage is charged for extra time incurred. Any delay which may occur outside the charterer's control, as transport to ship, is no defence for the charterer. Should, however, a strike or some change in circumstances of a like nature arise which makes the carrying out of the charter-party impossible, then the charter may be considered to be frustrated by delay.

When the charterer supplies the cargo, the master must take same on board with all reasonable speed – expressed in the term 'as fast as ship can load'. The supplying of the cargo is generally considered to mean supplying the cargo alongside the ship, or within reach of the ship's gear.

Lay days are qualified as excluding Sundays, Bank holidays, and public holidays, therefore the number of lay days from Thursday to the following Wednesday would be only six, and from Thursday to Wednesday at Eastertide only four days (Good Friday, Sunday, and Easter Monday all being excluded). It is advisable to be careful when dealing with a foreign country to see that religious festivals and local holidays are excluded in order to avoid loss of one or more lay days.

All terms and conditions of bills of lading issued under a charter-party are controlled by the charter-party terms, and the clauses of a charter-party overrule the terms of a bill of lading, unless bill of lading is endorsed to third party.

A simple time charter, as shown below, gives the formation of a charter-party.

IT IS MUTUALLY AGREED between . . . . Owner of the good ship . . . . . . classed . . . . . . Gross . . . . . . net . . . . . . now at . . . . and Messrs. . . . . as Charterers.

That said vessel being tight and staunch and in every way fitted for the contract in prospect is agreed to be delivered to the port of . . . . on . . . . or if not ready by the . . . . and to be redelivered in like good order and condition, fair wear and tear excepted at . . . . . or as near thereto as possible on . . . .

Hire is to be paid at the rate of . . . . . . per month, payment to be made in cash in London.

It is agreed that ship shall not be responsible for Act of God, Perils of the Sea, Queen's Enemies, Pirates, Rovers, Thieves, and Restraint of Princes of any kind whatsoever.

Time ceases to count in the case of a breakdown of machinery lasting for more than 24 hours, or for the purpose of dry-docking for inspection.

It is mutually agreed that vessel shall carry any lawful merchandise, not requiring special handling, loading or stowage, and shall trade within world-wide radius, ice-bound ports excepted, within Institute Warranty limits, providing that vessel shall always be afloat.

Owners to appoint Captain and Chief Engineer, but Charterers to provide stores, provisions, crew's wages, and maintenance.

Any bunkers on board at port of delivery to be purchased by Charterers at current prices at that place, and any bunkers on board at port of redelivery to be purchased by Owners at prices ruling at that port.

Owners to have a lien on cargo or freight for hire money due and not paid.

It is agreed that a commission of 5 per cent shall be paid to Brokers acting on behalf of Charterers.

. . . . Signature.

Date

8 Freight

Freight is the consideration payable to the carrier for the safe carriage and delivery of goods in a merchantable condition.

Charter-party freight and bill of lading freight differ in many respects, and these are discussed separately in order to prevent confusion.

Bill of lading freight is due on safe carriage and delivery of the goods. Many companies, however, demand freight in exchange for bills of lading, or freight to be paid within seven days of vessel's sailing. This is adopted in order to make collection easy and assured.

Freight on bill of lading shipments is calculated in three ways, weight of cargo, measurement of cargo, or, when the value is high, at *ad valorem* freight, the latter being chargeable at so much per cent on the declared value of the goods.

The carrier has the right of deciding whether the goods shall be carried at weight or measurement, whichever produces the highest freight. Whilst appearing at first glance to be to the advantage of the carrier, this is reasonably decided on the basis that heavy cargo will sink a vessel to her load line, long before the space is fully occupied, and light cargo will fill the space of the ship's holds and yet not bring the vessel down to her marks. Relationship of weight to measurement of cargo is dealt with under cargoes.

The greater number of Liner Conferences have now adopted the metric basis of freight calculation, namely per cubic metre or per tonne of 1000 kilos. As a matter of historic interest, until recently, the basis of calculating freight was on 40 cubic feet to a measurement ton or 20 cwt (of 2240 lb.) per weight ton. This now superseded basis had its origin in the fact that in olden times four hogsheads of wine constituted a 'tun', and occupied approximately 50 cubic feet. This 'tun' of 50 cubic feet, had by usage and custom, gradually altered to a ton of 40 cubic feet.

It must be mentioned however, that the measuring of cargo is often still conducted in feet and inches, and cubed up, then converted into metric figures for freighting purposes.

It may be considered that light cargoes, fine goods, provisions, etc., are charged on measurement, and heavy cargoes pay freight on their weight.

An example of this may be given: a case measuring 5 ft. x 4 ft. x 3 ft., produces 60 cu. ft., constituting 1½ tons measurement at 40 cu. ft. The actual weight of the case, however, may be 1 ton if filled with light goods or 2 tons if filled with heavy goods. In the first example there is excess of half a ton measurement over the weight, and the cargo becomes chargeable at measurement rate, whilst in the latter case there is an excess of half a ton weight, and the cargo therefore is rated at weight.

• For measuring cargo, exterior measurements are taken, fractions of an inch being counted as an inch on the first measurement, and dropped on the second measurement; for example, a case measuring 2 ft. 4½ in. x 3 ft. 6¼ x 6 ft. 8½ in., would be cubed as 2 ft. 5 in. x 3 ft. 6 in. x 6 ft. 9 in.

Cargo of uneven shape which loses space in stowing is chargeable on the actual space occupied, including the lost space. All space lost in such circumstances is termed broken stowage.

The accompanying illustration shows barrels (left) in order to make the concept of 'broken stowage' clear, but the student is more likely to come across drums (right), made of plywood, steel or plastic, where the loss of space will be slightly less. Broken stowage occurs in the spaces shaded. The shipowner, therefore, is entitled to charge for cubic space used, and may calculate it as if the cube of the barrel is the same at the top and bottom as the centre. Occasionally, however, an allowance of ⅙th is made on the cubic measurement when barrels are being shipped.

Freight on bill of lading shipments is usually charged according to tariff rates, which are fixed by the different conferences referred to in an earlier chapter. These rates of freight are adjusted from time to time.

The master has a lien on all goods for freight due, but not paid, and until these charges are paid he may retain cargo. The consignee is not entitled to receive the goods until the freight has been paid, and the shipowner is strictly not entitled to his freight until he has delivered the cargo, unless contract calls for freight in advance.

If the master delivers the cargo before payment of freight he may lose his lien, therefore he is entitled to claim his freight when he is *ready* to deliver.

Charter-party freight is fixed at an agreed rate for so much per ton (1015 or 1016 kilos) or other trade measure. Here there is no stipulation for weight or measurement cargo.

Charter-party freight is nearly always due on delivery of the cargo, and when the contract is silent as to the time for payment it is understood that freight is paid concurrently with delivery. The term 'Freight paid ton by ton delivered', must not be taken to mean what it literally says. Here a total of the day's work and cargo discharged is notified to the charterer who pays freight on that quantity.

Again, a carrier is not entitled to his freight until cargo is delivered, and in the event of the ship not reaching its port of discharge no freight may be claimed.

The shipowner is not entitled to claim *pro ratâ* freight for the part of the voyage he has carried the goods, but if the ship does not complete the voyage, the master may make arrangements to tranship the cargo to final port of discharge and thus earn his freight, all charges for such transhipment or forwarding being for his account.

There is an exception to this rule, however: if the consignee is notified that the ship has stopped short of its destination, and voluntarily agrees with the shipowner to take delivery at the intermediate port, then *pro rata* freight would become chargeable.

Whenever disputes occur regarding the weight of cargo carried, the person who requires the goods to be checked, must pay costs of such check-weighing.

In the case of damaged cargo, the shipowner is entitled to full freight provided he delivers the cargo; if, however, the goods are lost in transit no freight is earned.

In addition to the foregoing there are several other types of freight; these are:

Dead freight. Payment for space booked but not used. When by contract or charter-party space is booked for a definite quantity, and shippers fail to provide cargo, or do not provide the full amount agreed, then the owner is entitled to claim dead freight for unoccupied space.

The shipowner, however, is not entitled to place himself in a better financial position by receiving dead freight in excess of the actual freight he would have earned by the carriage of the goods. Dead freight is therefore calculated by the amount of cargo which should have been carried, but which in fact was not, at the agreed rate of freight, less all charges which would have been incurred by the owner in the carriage of the goods, i.e. loading and discharging expenses.

Dead freight is rarely demanded in cases where a shipper books space for a few cases in a berth shipment and fails to supply them.

Back freight. Freight charged for the return of goods which have not been accepted at port of delivery. Should a shipper forward goods to a consignee who refuses to take delivery, the owner may either exercise his lien — if freight has not been paid — and sell the goods, or return them to the shipper. The shipper is then charged with an additional amount of freight for their return, which is known as back freight.

Another form of back freight is when goods have been overstowed or overcarried, through a wrong mark appearing on the case. For example, goods intended for Montevideo, and port-marked 'Buenos Aires' would not be accessible at Montevideo, and would, therefore, have to be overcarried to Buenos Aires. There again back freight would be chargeable for the return of the goods from Buenos Aires to Montevideo, and if wrongly marked would be chargeable to the shipper.

If, however, goods have been wrongly stowed, and are overcarried, the mistake is the error of the carrier and no back freight becomes chargeable.

Lump sum freight. An agreed amount for the carriage of the goods, not based upon quantity. This freight is payable in full irrespective of the quantity carried or delivered.

For example: a shipper wishes a cargo of anything up to 4000 tons to be carried to a certain port, and agrees to pay the carrier the sum of £8000 for the carriage. He may, therefore, ship either 400 or 4000 tons and the freight paid still remains at the lump sum figure of £8000.

In order to earn this lump sum freight the shipowner must carry and deliver at least some of the cargo.

In the case of cargo short delivered, the receiver is only entitled to claim for the value of the cargo, and not for the freight unearned. Lump sum freight is payable irrespective of quantity delivered.

Freight of this nature is advantageous to a shipper who is uncertain of the quantity of cargo to be carried, as by making such an agreement, he can obtain a cheaper rate than if he shipped under a charter fixture.

Advance freight. Perhaps the most important type of freight, being payable in advance and recoverable only if the shipowner deliberately contributes to the loss. If the ship should sink or be a total loss on her outward trip or cargo be lost by an accepted peril, the cargo owner is unable to obtain the return of his freight if paid in advance.

It is a matter to be settled by the bill of lading conditions whether the freight paid on delivery of bills of lading constitutes advance freight or not. This can only be settled by reference to the clause relating to it in the bill of lading.

When charter-parties are fixed and a proportion of freight is payable in advance, this may be either advance freight, or payment on account of disbursements. If it is advance freight then in the case of a loss it is never returnable, but where it can be proved by the terms of the contract only to have been a payment on account for disbursements and other charges, then it does not come under this heading.

It is curious to note that if the agreement states that freight shall be paid in advance and it is not paid, and the vessel meets with disaster before such payment is made, the carrier is entitled to sue the shipper for payment of advance freight.

The most simple method of ascertaining whether freight is advance freight or not, is by finding who bears the insurance. If the shipper insures the freight, it is advance freight; if the shipowner bears the insurance, it is not advance freight.

Great care should be taken in dealing with this last type of freight.

Stoppage in transitu. The carrier has the right of stopping goods in transit if freight has not been paid when freight is to be paid within a stipulated time before delivery. He may instruct his master to hold or return the goods. Should the shipper himself have paid the freight and charges, and not have received payment from his consignee who refuses to pay, or becomes insolvent or bankrupt, he also may instruct the carrier to have the goods stopped until such time as he may notify him of receipt of the charges, or if there is no chance of his consignee paying for the goods then he may instruct the carrier to return same to him. In this case back freight would be chargeable to the shipper.

9 Liens

A lien is the right to hold property against the satisfaction of a claim.

Liens may be divided for the purpose of this chapter into two classes, the common law or possessory lien and the maritime lien.

A common law lien is enforceable under common law. By virtue of it a holder of goods may retain them until such a time as his charges are settled. He has no right to sell the goods, and except where the Merchant Shipping Act 1894 (Sects 492–501) allows them to be landed without loss, a shipowner has no right of lien once he has permitted the goods to be taken from the ship. Possession, actual or constructive, is essential to a common law lien.

The common law right to retain goods may be extended by statute or agreement.

A maritime lien is a claim on ship's tackle, ship, or cargo, also for settlement of charges incurred. It is not based on possession.

Speaking generally, liens are only enforceable on the actual subject which has caused the debt, and are not transferable. This, however, is overcome in relation to freight liens by the carrier including in his bill of lading a clause which gives him the right to spread his lien, and make it what may be termed a 'general' lien, whereby he may exercise his lien on goods other than those which incurred the debt or charges.

Liens are enforceable on cargo for freight, but it must be remembered that this does not include advance freight, dead freight, or freight payable after delivery.

Where a lien is exercised for freight, the shipowner may hold the cargo until the freight and charges are paid, and, as mentioned earlier, it is quite usual to find a clause in the bill of lading or charter-party expressing that such a lien be transferred or extended to other goods belonging to the same receiver (or shipper, whoever is due to pay such charges). This extension or generalization of lien must be according to the terms of the contract, and if such a condition is not mentioned therein the lien may not be transferred.

A lien cannot be exercised on advance freight because this of course is paid in advance, and there is no necessity for such a lien to be required.

In the same way, dead freight is usually excepted from liens. As already mentioned, dead freight is freight payable on space booked but not used, and the carrier has no object upon which he may exercise his lien.

Where payments for advance freight or dead freight have not been secured these charges may be applied by the terms of a general lien to other cargo belonging to the defaulting shipper.

When the terms of delivery are 'freight payable *after* delivery', then delivery must be made before freight is due, and in order to obtain the right to claim freight the carrier must lose the goods and also lose the lien.

Reference has been made to demise charter-parties, and it may be observed that by this type of charter-party the owner of a vessel has no representative on board the ship who is in a position of exercising a lien on cargo or ship for the payment of hire money due.

For general goods and perishable goods there is a slight variation in the application of a lien.

General goods must be retained for 90 days before they may be sold to satisfy the lien, during which time any offer of settlement must be accepted.

In the case of perishable goods, these may be sold immediately in order that the carrier has an object upon which he may exercise a lien. If the receiver of perishable cargo is not forthcoming, or his charges are not paid immediately the goods are ready to be landed, then, if the carrier wishes, such goods may be sold whilst they are in a saleable condition. The retention of fruit, for example, for the period of 90 days would be long enough to destroy the object upon which the carrier anticipates realization of his charges. It may be mentioned here that it is always the receiver of cargo who is responsible for ascertaining when the goods will be discharged, and there is no obligation on the part of the carrier to notify him of the arrival of the ship. It is always best in the interest of friendly relations between all parties that the carrier shall notify the receiver when the goods will be discharged from the vessel.

If goods are discharged from the ship into a warehouse, then the owner of such goods may claim them on tendering to the warehouse keeper or other responsible person, the charges incurred by the shipment plus warehouse expenses, and this gives to the warehouse keeper the right to deliver goods immediately.

It has been stated in cases in the past that a carrier may, if he so desires, use his ship as a warehouse by retaining cargo on board, and for such time that his ship is engaged as a 'warehouse' he may claim rent, to which he is legally entitled. Carriers usually prefer to discharge the goods rather than delay their vessels, and incidentally incur heavy expenses for dock charges.

After the period of 90 days has elapsed then the goods may be sold, such a sale being known as a compulsory sale. Before a compulsory sale takes place, the owner of the goods must be notified, if possible, and the sale advertised in at least two papers, and the goods sold publicly. The amount realized by such a sale is disposed of in the following manner:

Payment of customs and excise dues.
Expenses of the sale.

Payment of warehouse fees, and any expenses incurred in this
connection.
Landing charges.
Settlement of the lien.

It will be seen that sufficient cargo must be retained to satisfy all these
charges, otherwise the lien is not perfect. Should there not be sufficient
money realized by such a sale, then the person who exercises the lien is
consequently out of pocket, and has little recourse for the balance to the
late owner of the goods.

On the other hand, if after the lien is settled, and all the charges are
paid, there should be a balance over, then this amount remains the property
of the cargo owner, and must be handed to him.

Once a shipping agent has put the cargo into the carrier's hands, he
loses possession of such goods, and consequently upon failure of his
consignees to make payment, is debarred from exercising his right. He may,
however, make recourse by requesting the carrier to stop such goods or
return them in the event of freight or charges not being paid. As the
majority of agents send their documents forward through banking houses
this practice of stoppage *in transitu* (see p. 54) is generally rare, the banking
house holding the documents, or exercising their lien, until charges have
been paid to them.

Maritime liens are somewhat different from common law or possessory
liens, usually being incurred for service rendered, or for injury caused, or
again for breaches of foreign laws resulting in fines made upon the ship.

These maritime liens travel with the object upon which they are
enforceable (i.e. ship, tackle, or cargo), irrespective of the number of
persons through whose hands the object may pass. Reference to a bill of
sale for ships will show there the term 'free of incumbrances', which sets
out that there is no mortgage, or lien outstanding upon the ship. If a
purchaser of tonnage buys a ship and does not see that such a clause is in
his bill of sale, he may find there is a maritime lien upon the vessel, in
which case he, as the present owner, must make settlement or risk seizure.

A holder of a Bottomry Bond, or a Respondentia Bond, has a lien on
the ship and cargo respectively, for the settlement of his charges.

A bottomry bond is the document used when a loan is made to the
master, in exchange for which and by way of security he pledges his vessel,
that in the event of her returning to port or reaching her destination
settlement of the loan will be made, or the holder of the bond has the right
to exercise his lien, and seize the ship in lieu of payment. A respondentia
bond applies to a loan on the security of cargo alone, when the master is
unable to obtain sufficient money for his purpose against the pledging of
his owner's credit or vessel, in which case he may pledge the freight, and
finally the cargo.

Should a vessel be lost, when a lien is held either by way of bottomry
or respondentia, then the holder automatically loses his right of lien,

because the object upon which he has the power of exercising such lien has ceased to exist. It will be noticed by reference to the form of bottomry bond in the appendix that the holder of the bond is given settlement or right of lien only upon the safe arrival of the ship.

When a vessel is seized under a maritime lien, it may not be sold until such a time as action has been taken, and sanction has been given by a court of law for the vessel to be disposed of.

10 General Average

The law of general average is included in the law of every country engaged in maritime adventure, and dates back as one of the early, if not the earliest, laws in connection with shipping. Its principle is: 'That which is sacrificed for all, is borne in proportion by all interested in the adventure.'

The custom arose in olden times when merchants used to travel with their wares. If a disaster occurred where the saving of the vessel could only be avoided or overcome by one of the merchants sacrificing his wares, it was an understood thing that all the fellow travellers should make good the loss sustained by the merchant in order that such merchant should not ultimately suffer by his sacrifice.

The principles of general average were known in the merchant codes of the Cretans and the Romans, and were included in the Rhodian Law.

The definitions of general average to be considered are those in the York-Antwerp Rules, and the Marine Insurance Act 1906. General average is a distinct subject from marine insurance, but it is incorporated in the Marine Insurance Act as it is the practice of merchants and owners to insure against possible contributions to general average.

The York-Antwerp Rules state:

'There is a general average act, when and only when any extraordinary sacrifice or expenditure is intentionally and reasonably made or incurred for the common safety for the purpose of preserving from peril the property involved in a common maritime adventure.'

The Marine Insurance Act, Sect. 66 (2), states:

'There is a general average act where any extraordinary sacrifice or expenditure is voluntarily and reasonably made or incurred in time of peril for the purpose of preserving the property imperilled in the common adventure.'

The essential features are:

(1) *Extraordinary sacrifice.* The sacrifice must be extraordinary and not the sacrifice of articles by using them for the purpose for which they were provided, e.g. rockets and flares which are used for distress signals are provided for this purpose and are, therefore, not a general average expense.

(2) *Voluntary sacrifice.* The sacrifice must be a voluntary one, and where property is potentially lost it cannot be considered to have been sacrificed and is, therefore, not a general average act.

(3) *General.* The peril must be general, and the interest must be for all,

and not one party only, e.g. for the advantage of ship or cargo alone.

There are general average losses and general average expenditures.

A general average loss is a direct loss due to a general average act, such as jettison of cargo, damage to ship's engines, forcing ship off ground, or material burnt for fuel.

A general average expenditure is an expense incurred due to a general average act, as for example expenses of entering a port of refuge or of repairs, or of discharging and reloading cargo necessary for repair purposes.

The calculation of the amount lost or expended on the general average act in case of damage to a ship is based on the reasonable cost of repairing the vessel, less a deduction of 'new for old'. A shipowner having his vessel repaired due to a general average act is, after such repairs have been made, in a better position than he was before such general average act, because he has new material where previously there was only old, and consequently a deduction or allowance must be made for this. (See the comparison of the 1950 and 1974 Rules on this subject in Appendix B.)

Cargo is based on the market value of the goods at the port of destination on the last day of discharge. If goods are destroyed the consignee receives the market value of the goods less such expenses (landing charges, customs duty, etc.) as he would have been called upon to pay had the goods been delivered.

Where goods have been delivered damaged, then the amount payable is the difference between the net sound and net damaged value.

The shipowner is entitled to claim for freight which he has lost by reason of non-delivery, less all expenses that he would have incurred in the discharge of the cargo.

The interests which contribute to the general average fund are cargo, ship, and freight. Cargo is based on the gross arrived value less deduction for charges (freight, landing, etc.); ship, on the value of the vessel, either sound or damaged; freight, the gross amount at risk, less deductions for port and landing charges, etc.

No person claiming under general average is allowed to profit by such a loss, and may only receive compensation for the actual loss which he has suffered. In the case of a cargo owner who loses the whole of his cargo, he receives the value of the cargo less his proportion of the contribution to the fund for the amount of his lost cargo.

The settlement of a general average act is known as an adjustment, and the work entailed is very extensive and detailed. This work is carried out by *average adjusters.*

This adjustment should be carried out at the port of destination or the place of termination of the voyage. The adjustment may be drawn up elsewhere, but only provided it is done in the same manner as carried out at port of destination.

It is the duty of the shipowner to have the average adjustment drawn up, and until settlement of average payments has been made, the carrier has a lien on all cargo for contributions.

As the completion of an adjustment takes some considerable time, it is difficult for a carrier to exercise his lien, especially when the amount due is not known. The carrier, therefore, obtains from the consignee or owner of the cargo a signed bond, known as an average bond, stating that when the value of the loss has been ascertained he will pay his proportion. He also makes a deposit on account, for which he receives a 'deposit receipt', and the cargo is then released to him.

The collection of contributions and deposits is usually carried out by the shipowner, and these sums are paid into a 'general average account', which is a joint account, in the name of the shipowner and a representative of the cargo owners. The interest that is earned by this money whilst on deposit in the joint account is for the benefit of the depositors, and is included in the final statement.

Where the cargo owner has insured against general average losses the underwriter usually pays an amount equal to the cargo owner's proportion, and should there be any refund when settlement is made, this is refunded to the underwriter.

When the adjustment is complete copies are circulated to all parties concerned and the settlement is then made.

There are three 'Rules', 1924, 1950 and 1974. Although the 1924 Rules are not now in common use, they remain valid. It will be seen on reference to the appendix that only the most recent two sets of York-Antwerp Rules, the 1950 and 1974 codes are compared. Both codes are in operation, and the bill of lading or charter-party should be clearly worded stating under which code of rules settlement shall be effected.

The rule of interpretation at the commencement and the 1950 code, makes it clear that the 1950 Rules form a general average code in themselves and defines the relative functions of the lettered rules and numbered rules.

The 1950 and 1974 Rules are included in the appendix of this volume, and should be closely studied and comparison made between the two sets of rules.

11 The Master

The correct title for this person of authority is the 'master' of a ship, although many persons use the expression 'captain'. The term captain is applied only as a courtesy title, and is strictly a naval rank. (On large sailing ships of war during the 17th, 18th and early 19th centuries, the sailing 'master' was a separate individual from the naval Commanding Officer of the ship, who bore the title 'Captain'.) All documents now refer to him as the master of the ship, and never describe him in any other manner or style. The master has a special contract with his shipowners quite separate from that agreement for engaging the crew.

His duties are many. He is in absolute charge of his vessel, and in addition to being in control of his ship, may bury people. It has not been possible to trace the right of a master to conduct marriages. This would appear to be what might be described as legal fiction.

His authority is every extensive, and in the past was even more so than at present. As a matter of administrative convenience, the major part of the control is now vested in the marine superintendent and the shore staff of the vessel's managers.

Years ago when a vessel left her port of loading, she was not heard of again by the owners until she returned, there being no communication by telephone, wireless or cable, and consequently the master had to be entrusted with the ship's business, and the ship's management, and his authority was definitely extensive and gave him considerable powers. Now, however, by the intervention and introduction of these methods of communication, the owners may advise the master what to do, and where to go, may fix business at one end of the world for ports at the other end, and they have accordingly taken over the greater proportion of the business which was formerly transacted by the master. He is thus relieved of much of his past responsibility, and it is usually found that when encountering matters of a difficult nature he will cable or advise his owners and await their instructions.

It was in those early times of complete responsibility of the master that use of bottomry bonds and respondentia bonds was regularly made. When a master of a ship found that the freight he had earned and collected, and other moneys on board were insufficient to pay for charges he had incurred, then bottomry bonds were used, by which the ship was pledged against a loan. If the ship proved to be insufficient for this purpose then the cargo was also pledged by way of respondentia bonds. Now, however, within a few minutes large sums of money may be transmitted from one country to another, and the need for these documents has consequently decreased.

Apart from the powers of managing the ship's business, the master has supreme authority aboard his ship, and anything done to protect his vessel and save it from hazard including calling upon crew and/or passengers in case of need should be done. In the case of extreme emergency where the peril might endanger the ship, such as in the rare case of mutiny, any act of the master is regarded as one of self-defence, and he may call on all persons on board to render assistance (in a similar manner to police officers on land who may demand assistance in a time of danger from any person), failure to give such assistance constituting a crime.

A master has full authority to purchase necessary stores and equipment for his ship, and the charges for same are a charge against the owners, but goods which may be deemed unnecessary, although ordered by the master for the owners, may be chargeable to the master. He is only allowed to make purchases which are necessary and reasonable. What is 'a necessary' may be ascertained by determining whether the owner, being a prudent man, would have acted in a similar manner had he been on board at the time.

The master may pledge either his own or his owner's security for the purpose of raising money, and when this is insufficient he may resort to the use of a bottomry bond or a respondentia bond. The pledging of cargo, however, must not be undertaken unless the conditions are so severe as to warrant such an action. The master as bailee of the cargo has only the custody and safe carriage of the goods, and he may never, unless in a time of danger, interfere with the cargo owner's property, unless this is a direct benefit to the cargo owner's interest in the adventure. The pledging of cargo to ensure completion of the voyage would come within cargo owner's interests.

When a master receives orders which may be regarded as unlawful then he is not bound to act upon them.

All bills of lading are signed by or on behalf of the master, and it is the duty of the master to see that goods are on board before he signs the documents, and also that they conform with the description in the bill of lading regarding the 'apparent good order and condition'. Should he sign for goods which are not as per description then he is fully responsible for any claims which may be made.

The correct time for signing bills of lading is when the goods are received, but as this is a practical impossibility, and the master's time is of greater value to the company, the bills of lading are usually signed for on behalf of the master by one of the company's representatives, and issued from their offices. This, however, does not relieve the master from responsibility in this connection.

In a time of danger to the ship, the master has full authority to act as agent for both shipowner and cargo owner, and may then be considered to have implied authority for all matters, including the disposal of cargo. He may jettison goods and do such other acts which may benefit the adventure as a whole without fear of being held responsible, and may also, when cargo is damaged or in the case of perishable cargo which has deteriorated, dispose of the goods to the best of his ability on behalf of the owner of the cargo. In such cases, he may be found to be exceeding his authority unless he acts with considerable discretion.

His liability is practically unlimited, and he is fully responsible to the owners as their agent for any default or neglect. For example, in the case of deviation, if a master deviates without authority of the owners, then he is fully responsible and may be sued by the owners for any loss incurred.

In the case of illness the charges for attendance and any expenses incurred are for account of the owners, and in the event of death the expenses for the burial must also be for account of the owners without deduction from salary.

12 The Crew

The master is the authority in command of a ship, and he has a special contract with his shipowners. The shipowner is now the contracting party and his office is accorded a legal position by being specified as 'Crew Engagement Offices'.

All other persons (including officers) and ratings must be engaged according to the regulations of the Department of Trade and must sign the 'crew agreement', and when doing so they also agree to comply with the new Code of Conduct, when making their contract with the owners' office for the intended voyage.

The new Code of Conduct came into force on 1 January 1979, or on any subsequent date of the renewal of a crew engagement. It applies to all officers (including cadets) and ratings, serving in a UK-registered ship on an approved Crew Agreement and subject to National Maritime Board conditions. It has been agreed between the employers (the shipowners), the unions, and the Department of Trade.

There are a few exceptions to the general application of the Code of Conduct, for instance a crew who have shares in the voyage or a non-UK-registered ship.

The basis of the new Code of Conduct is that by signing the Crew Agreement the seaman agrees to conduct himself reasonably rather than having discipline imposed on him by law. Fines as specified in the 1972 Merchant Shipping Act are withdrawn.

The crew agreement contains the following particulars:

(1) Nature of the voyage and length of time, or period of engagement.
(2) Number of crew, and the capacity in which each serves.
(3) Amount of wages to be paid.
(4) Time of commencement of work.
(5) Scale of provisions to be supplied.

The crew agree by signing the agreement to serve, obey, and be diligent in carrying out their duties, and in a time of danger to do everything possible to save the ship, without regard to the work or without expectation of extra pay for the extra work undertaken in such a time. Should they refuse such extra duties in a time of stress then such refusal may be deemed an act of wilful disobedience.

If an offence is committed by a crew member of sufficient seriousness to warrant in accordance with a predetermined procedure an entry of the offence at the time in the ship's Official Log, he may either find himself dismissed from the ship and the company, or the diciplinary Committee of the National Maritime Board may recommend to the Department of Trade that his Certificate of Competancy be suspended or cancelled and/ or that his Discharge Book be withdrawn and that he be excluded from the Merchant Navy. This, in the extreme case, is the ultimate sanction.

There is no necessity for a master to sign on any sailor as a member of his crew who does not understand English sufficiently to carry out the orders of the officers.

The nature of the voyage and the duration is usually stipulated in a manner sufficient to cover all time taken on the voyage, for the crew may, on the termination of their period of engagement, demand their wages and close the contract. This, of course, would often leave the owner in an awkward position, especially if the contract terminated at a remote or inconvenient spot. The nominal period is for six months or for one or two years but crew members may demand to be paid off in one year.

The number of crew and amount of wages is inserted in the agreement, such wages being paid according to scale fees.

The date of commencement of work, and provisions supplied are also inserted.

Fining seamen for breaches of peace or failure of duty has been abolished, as has the old-fashioned corporal punishment.

A seaman on signing the agreement may leave a proportion of his wages to his own account with a savings bank, or to whom he wishes. Allotments are payable either monthly, half-monthly or weekly from the time when wages are earned until the voyage is terminated, but allotments cease when a seaman leaves his ship.

When required, advance notes are obtained by crew members to pay for 'necessaries' for an intended voyage, and are repaid out of wages.

The seaman has a maritime lien on the ship for the payment of wages. This lien, however, does not extend to the cargo.

Expenses by way of hospital or medical attention incurred by the seamen are payable by the owners of the ship without deduction from the wages of the seamen.

The engagement of the crew terminates if the vessel is sold. As will be seen from chapter 16, when an owner sells a vessel he has no right to transfer the crew, and must therefore terminate the agreement. The crew usually have the option of signing a fresh agreement with the new owners.

Where a vessel becomes a wreck or is disabled and unable to proceed upon her voyage, then the owners of the ship may claim the cancellation of the agreement by reason of the fact that the voyage is frustrated, and it is impossible to fulfil or continue it.

In the event of a sudden cancellation of the voyage through wreck or other termination of the adventure, the seaman is entitled to claim compensation by way of payment of wages for a period of two months, provided that during that period he has not become otherwise employed.

When a seaman becomes what is known as a distressed seaman he is entitled to repatriation. He may become distressed by being wrecked, or left behind in the case of illness, or, within certain regulations, if he deserts. All distressed seamen may claim return to proper return ports at the expense of the owner in whose employ they become distressed.

A simple example of repatriation is if a seaman is signed on in the United Kingdom and discharged in a foreign country, he is entitled to be returned (or repatriated) to the United Kingdom.

In the case of Lascars, these must always be returned to India, and may never be discharged in any other country than their own. Lascar crews are under the control of a Serang, who is responsible for their behaviour. Lascars do not sign to comply with the Code of Conduct.

The cost of repatriation includes maintenance whilst waiting for the ship upon which they are to be returned, and proper accommodation and maintenance on board ship.

Masters of all British vessels if accommodation is available are bound to accept on board their ships on request, distressed seamen, and also to provide suitable accommodation for each of them. Seamen being repatriated are not allowed to work in any way for the master who is returning them, and if they undertake any duty on the homeward ship they must be signed on the agreement, and the repatriation charges immediately cease to be for account of the original owner.

The 1979 Merchant Shipping Act is a most important piece of legislation and deals with a number of points quite apart from crew relations. Students are advised to obtain copies of the act and to study it carefully.

13 Recent Legislation

The Department of Trade (previously, The Board of Trade) has hitherto been the Department of State charged with responsibilities in connection with Merchant Shipping in general, and its authority has been exercised by specially qualified officers with deep knowledge of the industry's day-to-day problems and those of they who work on ships.

Within the scope of the appropriate regulations much of their power is discretionary and it speaks volumes for the wisdom of the manner in which their authority has been and is exercised that so little of it is audibly challenged. The Department has power to issue and/or modify regulations governing matters on shipboard. The Department's Surveyors and Technical Inspecting Officers are generally very highly thought of.

The Department of Trade's powers have always extended to the authority to set up enquiries into accidents to or aboard ships, and of course to the loss of ships, or to establish what may be the actual or probable cause of any loss or damage or injury to personnel. Such inquiries often have the powers of Courts and their findings are crucial. These Merchant Shipping Acts should be studied so as to gather an appreciation of the scope of the work covered by them.

The Merchant Shipping Acts

There have been several Merchant Shipping Acts of various dates, parts of which have been amended from time to time, leaving unaltered other portions of the respective acts as originally brought into law.

The purpose of these Acts, apart from the earlier ones, has been to take account of changes in the Law brought about by historical or technical developments, and the improvements, progress and increased safety in the business of shipowning and those who have their business in ships.

These can usefully be studied, but it is recommended that this should only be done after consulting the Tables of repealed Sections and Supplementary Acts.

Recent Acts and Statutory Instruments are:

Merchant Shipping (load lines) Act 1967
Merchant Shipping (tonnage) (amendment) Regulations 1967
Merchant Shipping (tonnage) (amendment) Regulations 1972

Merchant Shipping (tonnage) (amendment) Regulations 1975
Merchant Shipping Notice, M.770, 1976 Measurement of certain Yachts.
Merchant Shipping (tonnage) Regulations 1977
These are concerned with the measurement of ships as a means of determining their tonnages, and the Statutory Instrument 1967, No. 172 with reference to the new Tonnage Mark is important in this connection.

Merchant Shipping Act 1970

This act is almost wholly concerned with matters affecting ships crews etc. It reinforces safeguards for the basic safety and welfare of seamen, and regulates the various authority's under which disciples or actions could be or were imposed, and the extent of them.

The provisions governing crew members' wages, allotments, permitted deductions etc., have been strengthened for the better protection of the interests of seamen.

Merchant Shipping Act 1974

This is concerned with the problem of oil pollution of the seas and navigable waters, and the setting up of a fund to deal with claims for compensation.

It also calls for the strengthening of safety regulations in respect of submersible apparatus and contains modifications of parts of the Merchant Shipping Act 1970 regarding misconduct by persons or seamen on a ship. The schedules accompanying the act also lay down further rules regarding surveys and inspection of tankers.

Merchant Shipping (Crew Accommodation) Regulations 1978

These came into force in 1979.

Merchant Shipping Act 1979

This deals with a variety of shipping subjects, e.g. pilotage, and kindred matters; carriage of passengers and luggage by sea; liability of shipowners and salvors; pollution; safety and health on ships; discipline; Department of Trade — Inspectors and their powers; death on ships; miscellaneous; etc., and seven schedules, the last one dealing with repealed sections of previous acts.

Merchant Shipping (Sterling Equivalents) (Various Enactments) Order 1980; Statutory Instrument No. 280, 1980

The purpose of this statutory instrument, and of similar instruments in the recent past and any to follow, has been to define the position in relation to gold francs and equivalent Sterling.

The gold franc concerned is not a 'coin' but is simply a unit of value and consists of 65.5 milligrammes of gold of millesimal fineness 900'. It was named after the French Prime Minister, M. Poincaré, who held office in 1928. It is often referred to as the 'Poincaré gold franc'.

On occasions since that time, attempts have been made, by way of

International Conventions and the resultant Protocols, to stabilize the value of sums involved in the legislation of various countries, signatories to the Conventions. Some of the international agreements have endured for quite a period, but in the long run they have all been defeated by the widely variable value of gold as a medium of exchange.

The above Statutory Order covers the following:

Merchant Shipping (Liability of Shipowners and Others) Act 1958
Carriage of Goods by Sea Act 1971
Section 4 (4) of Merchant Shipping (Oil Pollution) Act 1971, as amended by section 9 of Merchant Shipping Act 1974 and by section 1 (7) of Merchant Shipping Act 1974, and by Unfair Contract Terms Act 1977, and all other powers enabling the Secretary of State in that behalf.

The Sterling equivalents have been calculated by reference to the special drawing right (SDR) value of a gold franc converted into Sterling at the current market rates; the SDR is based on a basket of 16 major world currencies.

14 The Ship

The history of the world shows us that as far back as it is possible to trace, there has always been shipping in some shape or form, and whilst many of these old records may be of little value, there is no doubt that merchants owned ships and traded in regular routes some thousands of years ago.

Reference is made in Chapter 27 of the Acts of the Apostles to the vessel upon which Paul made his journey to Rome, and it states that there were two hundred and seventy-six persons on board the vessel, including crew and passengers. From this reference it will be easy to obtain some idea of the size of the vessels which as long ago as that were carrying out a passenger trade in the Eastern Mediterranean.

For an earlier reference to the beginning of this vast mercantile marine, we have, of course, the savage who was reputed to have noticed skins of dead animals and logs floating down the river, and to have discovered the value of transport by sitting upon these moving objects, then when standing he found that the pressure of the wind increased his speed, which produced the origination of the sail. This all, however, is a matter of great supposition.

We find, however, records of early ships, and these may be divided into sections, as Egyptian ships, which were propelled by a large paddle at the rear of the vessel; Phoenician ships, which were equipped with both oars and rudder; and the Greek and Roman fleets with their warlike vessels equipped with fighting gear and built-in rams.

When these early vessels were engaged in warfare which meant hand to hand fighting, it was discovered that by raising the ends of the ship, platforms could be built and used as castles or towers, from which vantage points large portions of rock could be hurled with ease into the enemy vessel. This gave the early name of the raised portion of a vessel, i.e. 'forecastle'.

It was not, however, until the sixteenth century that the three-master became known, and it was also about this period that the two-decker ship came into use; also, by the ingenuity of the fighting men, the cannon was introduced to the sea, and this meant building a heavy platform upon which these guns might rest, with the result that in a short time the two-decker ship was built and generally adopted, the top deck bearing the battery or cannon, and the under deck holding the rowers or oarsmen.

In this chapter it is intended to deal only very lightly with the origin

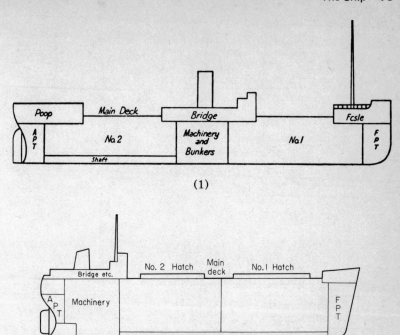

(1)

(2)

and types of vessels, and certainly not to cover any technical points with regard to construction or propulsion.

From the wooden ship developed the composite type of ship, which consisted of a vessel built of wood on an iron framing. This in due course gave way to the iron ship, many of which by reason of their great solidity are still in existence, a number of this type of vessel still being classified in Lloyd's Register.

From the iron ships a move was made to steel vessels, which proved to be equally as strong and by no means as heavy or as thick as the iron type.

In dealing with the different types of ships, there is the *single decker*, or sometimes known as self-trimming ship, which is constructed with one-depth holds only, division being made by bulkheads throughout the length of the ship. This type of vessel, two examples of which are illustrated above, is very useful in trades for the carriage of bulk cargoes. The large bulk carrier and the bulk/oil vessel are specialized developments of the single deck ship, and have grown very substantially in size and increased in speed.

The *'tween deck ship* or *two decker* provides more under-deck space for cargo and has an additional deck built under the main deck. This type of vessel, a sketch of which is shown on page 74 (No. 3), is used for cargoes of a heavyweight nature, or for cargoes of small cube.

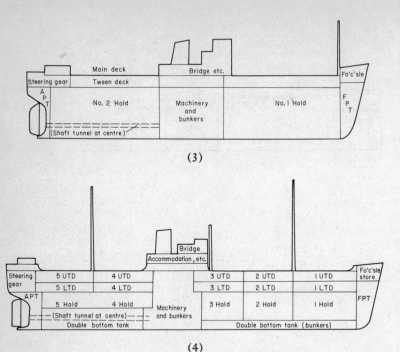

(3)

(4)

'Tween decks may be divided into upper and lower 'tween decks as shown in the sketch No. 4.

Heavy lifting ships. These are ordinary cargo vessels, either single- or multi-deck ships, specially strengthened, and fitted with heavy cranes or derricks.

Most conventional cargo liners can handle 50 or 60 tons but there are many ships capable of dealing with considerably heavier lifts with their own gear.

It must not be forgotten that many ports are equipped with heavy cranes, either fixed or floating, and some of these ports demand that their cranes be used to deal with heavy lifts within their juridiction. However, in arranging to deal with heavy lifts it depends upon the destination of the cargo concerned as to whether it can successfully be off-loaded. In considering heavy lifts, there are a number of floating cranes with enormous capacity, either towed or with their own propulsion, and capable of operating at sea, but such heavy floating cranes should not be confused with heavy lifting ships.

Container ships, because of the variety of sizes, are very different in type. Basically, as their name implies, they are built to carry containers (see Chapter 20) but they also range from the small vessel, having their below-deck spaces as a buoyancy chamber carrying their load on deck, through a number of vessels carrying containers under deck and on deck, say a Mediterranean trader with 80 or so containers, up to the ships carrying between 1100 and 2800 containers on long distance voyages.

Some of these large and fast container ships also have a Ro-Ro facility enabling them to accept cargo offering on specially designed trailers, such as very heavy lifts or large awkward shaped pieces much beyond the size or weight limits of an ordinary container.

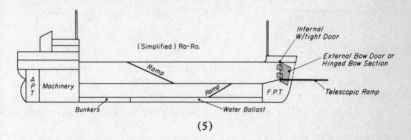

(5)

Roll on—roll off (Ro-Ro) ships are of many sizes (5), but common to all is they can accept vehicles on their wheels, carrying cargo or not, through or over ramps by means of bow or stern doors, or occasionally doors in their sides. These ramps or doors are usually complemented by further water-tight doors behind them as a safety measure.

The flush deck type is really a single or 'tween deck ship with the poop, bridge and forecastle combined in a continuous superstructure.

Coastal ships are single-deck, and usually single-hold ships with the engines built aft, providing the largest possible hatch openings in the smallest available space. These vessels are mostly used for coastal trades, and near continental ports.

Tank ships are vessels built specially for the carriage of liquids in bulk, such as acids, oil and/or derivatives, molasses, etc. *Gas carriers* are tankers of a very highly specialized type which carry gases in liquified form. Instead of the usual holds these vessels are fitted out with tanks for the direct reception of cargo, as may be seen in the sketch below.

It is to be noted that the type of ship to be adopted is determined by the following:

(1) The trade in which a vessel is to be engaged.

(2) The question of draught, together with tonnage, so that at times the deepest draught can be obtained, and at other times, when draught is unimportant, there is a maximum cargo capacity.

Refrigerator vessels are vessels used for the carriage of frozen and/or chilled cargoes, such as fruit, meat, etc., and have certain or all of their holds insulated, usually with granulated cork, glass fibre or other efficient insulating material, and equipped with refrigeration plant. Vessels with small refrigeration apparatus and rather limited insulated space (relative to their total cargo capacity) which are only used when perishable cargo

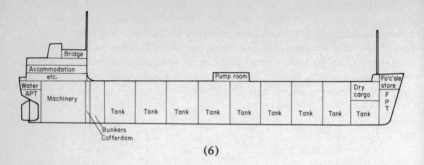

(6)

is carried must not be confused with or termed refrigerator vessels.

The general tendency is for the specialized ships to become larger and faster (except for those restricted by port limitations as mentioned before), while 'conventional' ships remain at about their present size with only a minor increase in speed.

The subject of the engines of a ship is beyond the scope of this book, and it is sufficient to mention that propulsion of ships is either by means of steam (this being generated by burning coal or oil under boilers) or by internal oil combustion engines. Ships with this latter type of engine are known as motor vessels.

Coal burning ocean going steam ships are now comparatively few, oil firing having almost wholly taken the place of coal as a fuel. The reasons are basically, the more convenient disposition of bunker space (for instance in the double bottom tanks) with consequent increase in available cargo space, and the cleaner and speedier operation of bunkering. To bunker a coal burning ship almost certainly meant moving the ship to a special coaling berth, being time consuming and inconvenient, whether it occurred after loading cargo or before. It was also a relatively dirty, dusty operation with the necessity of cleaning ship when it was complete. But with oil bunkering, be it from shore pipeline or re-fuelling lighter alongside, the task can be easily and cleanly conducted whilst cargo operations are going on at the same time.

World supply conditions of oil fuel(s) and heavy increases in prices have led to consideration of alternative sources of power for propulsion such as nuclear engines, also some success has been recently attained in the better combustion of fine coal in land based installations. Whilst conditions are very different at sea, the possibility remains that coal may return at some future date as a fuel for powering ships' engines. Should the technical problems of burning fine coal be successfully overcome for use under sea-going conditions, it may also bring in some very much better and cleaner ways of bunkering.

Another look is being taken at sailing ships. This is concentrated at the moment on improving sails, together with much easier hoisting and lowering of them. Auxiliary engines for propulsion on windless days and to provide power for loading and unloading cargo will be provided.

The chief centres of merchant shipbuilding in Britain are the Clyde, Mersey, Tyne, Wear and Belfast. The UK shipbuilders in the past produced much of the world's tonnage but this share has now been reduced and other countries such as Denmark, Sweden, Holland, Germany, Spain, South Korea, United States and Japan, also many countries of the Soviet Block have all increased their production and modernized their shipyards. A point has now been reached where, temporarily, total shipbuilding capacity exceeds current demand.

For a vessel to start trading she must be seaworthy and fit. It is the owner's duty to provide a ship that is 'tight, staunch and fit in every way for the voyage in prospect'. A ship need not be registered or classified with the registration societies such as Lloyd's Register, Bureau Veritas, or the American Bureau, but she must have some certification of compliance with national standards and regulations both as to design and materials, as without such it would be difficult, for instance to insure the ship.

In addition the vessel may be unseaworthy apart from build, etc., if she is under-manned, under-equipped, or not fit for the carriage of cargo. (See unfitness as defined on page 31 *ante*.)

Owing to the agitation of Samuel Plimsoll, who entered Parliament in 1868, the Government introduced in 1870 a bill upon the subject of load lines. This bill was withdrawn, and in 1871 an act was passed dealing with defective vessels. In 1873 a Royal Commission was appointed with the result that an act was passed in the same year. Another act was passed in 1875 upon the subject, and again repealed in 1876 by another act. Finally, in 1890, an act was passed, making it compulsory for all British vessels over 80 tons net register, with the exception of coastal boats and fishing boats, to have a line painted on the side of the vessel, and the vessel is not allowed to load more than will sink the ship to this mark. These provisions, it may be observed, were contained in Sect. 438 of the Merchant Shipping Act 1894, which was subsequently still further adjusted by the Merchant Shipping (Safety and Loadline Conventions) Act of 1932.

Under the 1967 Act fresh legislation was passed and new loadlines were allotted so that all vessels came under the new ruling.

The marking of the load line was a preventive measure whereby a carrier was not allowed to endanger the lives and property on board by overloading his vessel. The necessity for the step has been emphasized over and over again, when on loss of a vessel and loss of life it has been proved that these regulations have not been carried out.

Section 10 of the Merchant Shipping Act 1906, relating to timber, has been withdrawn and all ships carrying a deck load of timber have a special timber marking allotted to them. So long as the seasonal timber marking is not submerged, there is no limit to the quantity of deck cargo, with the exception that in winter time the height of deck cargo must not exceed one-third of the breadth of the ship.

The seasons to which the markings apply are Tropical (T), Summer (S),

Winter (W), and Winter North Atlantic (WNA). Some zones of the world are marked as seasonal, i.e. varying at times between winter and summer or tropical and summer. The world has been mapped off into sections showing where these seasons apply and the map is published under Board of Trade Rules and Orders No. 96 (Loadlines).

All ships must be loaded so that in every zone through which they pass the corresponding seasonal loadline must not be submerged and in some cases where voyages traverse two or three zones it is interesting to study which marking will apply.

The markings are as follows:

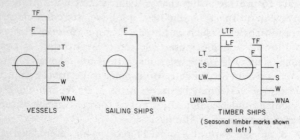

Metrication and feet and inches can sometimes be seen on alternative sides of bow and stern of draft marks on some ships.

A loadline certificate is issued at the time of the assignment and must be presented at times of clearance at customs. The granting of a certificate is conditional upon the ship undergoing periodical survey.

Freeboard is the distance measured amidship from the load line to the freeboard deck of a vessel (maindeck in single or 'tween deck vessels). The penalties for overloading are severe. The master has full authority to see that his marks are not submerged.

If, for example, it was agreed to load a vessel, and on the stipulated amount of tonnage being placed on board the vessel the master found that his marks were submerged (with a 'correction' for density, i.e. the specific gravity of sea water), he would have full authority, irrespective of the charter-party conditions, to demand that sufficient cargo should be taken off his vessel to comply with the load line regulations.

For a *mercantile ton*, or *freight ton*, the basis is 40 cubic feet per ton, but in measuring tonnage of ships the basis is 100 cubic feet.

Gross tonnage is the number of tons in units of 100 cubic feet of the total space enclosed in the vessel. *Net tonnage* is the measurement of the ship in units of 100 cubic feet of the enclosed spaces of the ship, excluding such spaces as are used for machinery, navigation and crew stores space; in other words, spaces allocated for the navigation of the ship are deducted, the approximate ratio of gross to net tonnage being about 3 : 2, although this, of course, must vary in individual cases.

Under deck tonnage is the measurement of the ship in units of 100 cubic feet of all parts under the main or tonnage deck of the vessel; this measurement does not, as in gross tonnage, include the poop, bridge, forecastle, or deck houses.

Vessels' *dead weight* is the number of tons (measured by 2240 lb.) required to sink the vessel in the water to her load line. The dead weight includes cargo, bunkers and stores.

Deadweight cargo capacity is the weight available for cargo after all other allowances have been made.

Displacement tonnage is the weight of water displaced measured in tons of 2240 lb, and is the effective weight of the structure in the condition in which the measurement takes place, i.e. light weight, or loaded weight. The loaded displacement, less the deadweight, is the light weight of the ship. The displacement tonnage is the more normal method of defining the tonnage of ships of war.

Other points of the ship will be dealt with in chapter 15.

It should be remembered that the whole of the rules and regulations for live-saving apparatus, regarding life-belts, life-boats, etc., are under the control of the Department of Trade, and this important section of the ship's equipment is dealt with and inspected entirely by that Government body.

Abbreviations of ship type titles

ARTUBAR— Articulated tug-barge.

BOS   — Barges on ship (variant of LASH and SeeBee, but with a different concept of stowage.)

Flo Con — Floating containers.

LASH   — Lighter(s) aboard ship.

Panamax — Maximum permitted size for passage through the Panama Canal.

OBO   — Ore/Bulk/Oil.

OSO   — Ore/Slurry/Oil.

Ro-Ro   — Roll on—Roll off.

SeeBee — Similar to LASH, but handling barges up to twice the size of previously.

15 Lloyd's Register of Shipping

Lloyd's Register of Shipping is a voluntary association of shipowners, shipbuilders, engine builders and underwriters which exists primarily for the purpose of surveying and classifying ships of any nationality and disseminating this information through the medium of the annual publication of Lloyd's Register of Ships, which contains in addition to details of classed ships particulars of all known seagoing merchant ships of 100 tons gross and above. There are other classification societies also operating with like purpose e.g. Det Norske Veritas, Registro Italiano and the American Bureau of Shipping, etc., but as nearly 79.17% of British tonnage and approximately 27.85% of the worlds tonnage (both as at 7/79) hold the classification of Lloyd's Register, and it is the only wholly independent classification society, it is proposed to deal with the work of that institution.

Its foundation, like those of the great Marine Insurance Corporation of Lloyd's, were laid in Lloyd's Coffee-house, which was situated in Tower Street in the City of London in 1688 and afterwards moved to Lombard Street. Here the proprietor, Mr Edward Lloyd, finding his establishment much frequented by underwriters, catered for his clients by collecting and publishing such information as was available regarding the ships they might be called upon to insure; and there is little doubt that the old Underwriters Registry which was founded in 1760 emerged from this source.

The oldest copy of a Register of Shipping — as far as can be ascertained — is one in the possession of Lloyd's Register of Shipping, bears the date 1764—65—66, for which period it was evidently current, and it is on permanent loan to the British Museum. This book was the 'Underwriters' Register' or 'Green Book', the letters A E I O U being employed for designating the several classes, while the letters G, M, and B (good, middling and bad) describe the condition of the equipment.

In the 1775—6 edition there first appeared the now familiar class 'A 1' which has passed into everyday language as symbolic of excellence.

Towards the end of the eighteenth century, the shipowners, dissatisfied with an alteration in the method of classification in the Green Book, started their own Register, which was known as the 'Shipowners' Register' or 'Red Book'. In almost everything but name the new Register was a replica of the old, and for over thirty years intense rivalry was maintained, greatly to the detriment of the Registries, which fell into disrepute. Funds dwindled to vanishing point as subscribers fell away, and in 1833 the Committee of Lloyd's, fearing that the shipping community might be left without a Register at all, sought the basis of an agreement for amalgamation. A provisional committee was formed for the purpose, drawn from representatives of Lloyd's and the London General Shipowner's Society from whose deliberations emerged a reconstituted society to be known as Lloyd's Register of British and Foreign Shipping.

Now, for the first time, the survey and classification of shipping was placed on a sound basis. Well-qualified surveyors were appointed at most of the principal ports in the United Kingdom under a Committee of Management in London drawn from elected representatives of the underwriters at Lloyd's, shipowning members of the London General Shipowners' Society and merchants; the income of the reconstituted Society was safeguarded by the application of approved scales of fees for surveys payable by owners seeking classification and the Register Book was made public and more easily accessible to all by a sweeping reduction in its price.

Rules and regulations governing the construction and maintenance of shipping were laid down and afterwards added to with each new development of marine and propulsion technology; and at the present day the rules of Lloyd's Register are universally recognized as the standard of best practice in merchant ship design principles and marine engineering. From wood to iron, iron to steel, sail to steam, and steam to motor, it has served as a clearing house of experience in the formulation of new rules and has through the past century grown from a London Register, first to a National Register, and afterwards to an International Register.

It cannot be too clearly emphasized however, that Lloyd's Register of Shipping and the Corporation of Lloyd's are quite distinct bodies, and the Surveyors to Lloyd's Register should not be confused with 'Lloyd's Agents', who are the representatives of the Corporation of Lloyd's.

Lloyd's Register of Ships now contains the names and particulars of over 70,000 vessels, and the following is a description of its present contents, which are in constant reference by underwriters as to the vessels they may be called upon to cover, and by shipowners and shippers in verifying particulars of ships offered for sale, charter or use.

Since 1975 Lloyd's Register has used computerized methods in producing the Register Book. Computer files of comprehensive data have been created and, in association with the Corporation of Lloyd's, an extensive information service is now available to the shipping community throughout the world.

In 1980 the Register of Ships consists of three volumes, Red (A–G), Black (H–O), and Green (P–Z), in which full particulars concerning ships classed with Lloyd's Register are recorded; also particulars of all known seagoing merchant ships in the world, and of all ships trading on the North American Lakes, of 100 tons gross and above. Measurements used throughout the Register are in metric units, except where otherwise indicated in the Key.

In a further volume of the Register additional information is published of ships or installations which hold the Lloyd's Register classification covering ship-borne barges, floating docks, refrigerated cargo installations, refrigerated cargo containers, refrigerated stores and container terminals.

A separate volume devoted to information about Off-Shore Units and Submersibles is published.

The Register is kept up to date by means of cumulative monthly supplements recording all amendments and the details of new ships. It is the only Register in the world to update all 70,000 ships entries as necessary.

The Appendix to the Register contains shipbuilders with existing ships they have built; marine-engine builders and boilermakers; dry and wet docks; telegraphic addresses and codes used by shipping firms; and lists of marine insurance companies. The separately published list of shipowners contains a list of owners and managers of ships recorded in the Register with their fleets, together with lists of former names of ships and compound names.

A brief description of the particulars found in the Register will be of interest.

Column (1)

Identity No., Universally known as the 'L.R number' for update index and reference purposes, and may also be used for cabling purposes, remains the same for each ship regardless of name changes and ultimate fate.

Call sign. This is assigned to ships by international authority for identification purposes and consists of a combination of letters or, in some cases, letters and numerals.

Official No., of the ship's Register. This number is allotted by and recorded on the Official Register of the country to which a vessel belongs. In the United Kingdom official numbers are allotted by the Registrar General of Shipping and Seamen.

Navigational aids. Particulars are given of any navigational aids with which the ship is fitted. The abbreviations used (e.g.) Rdr for 'radar') are self-explanatory and are explained in the 'Key' at the beginning of the Register of Ships.

Column (2)

Vessel's name. The current name of the vessel, and immediately underneath is found any other name she may have had previously (since 1932 the year of such change is also shown), thus giving a continuous history of the ship. It contain the name of the registered owner(s) of the ship. This may be – as often is the case – the name of the managing owner. Also shown in this column are the managers (if any), flag, and port of registry. The port of registry may be any port at which the owners may desire to register their vessel provided that port has an established Custom House or other registration facility and the flag shows the nationality of the ship.

Column (3)

Contains particulars of the ship's gross and net tonnage(s) and her summer deadweight(s).

Column (4)

Contains classification particulars. Classification may be well described as the comparison with an ideal standard. The class 100 A1 is defined in the Rules of Lloyd's Register in the following words:

This class will be assigned to seagoing ships built in accordance with the Society's Rules and Regulations for the draught required.

The Maltese cross (✛) preceding the 100 A1 notation indicates that the entire construction of the ship was under the inspection of Lloyd's Register surveyors.

The figure '1' indicates that her equipment of anchors, cables etc., is in good and efficient condition.

Ships are also classed for special or restricted service, shown in the Register by a class notation under the character of class, and in these cases the structure and arrangements are subject to special approval.

The hull and machinery classification are interdependent, the latter being shown as LMC for Lloyd's Register ships. The addition of a cross (✛) means that the engines and boilers were constructed under the inspection of Lloyd's Register surveyors.

The notation 'Lloyd's RMC' indicates that the ship holds a Refrigerating Machinery Certificate issued by Lloyd's Register and that details of the classification and refrigerating installation are in the Register Book. For classed vessels will also be found the latest dates of Special Surveys prescribed by Lloyd's Register rules, details of other surveys appearing in the Survey Dates Supplement. Some mention should be made here as to the withdrawal or expunging of a vessel's class. If an owner requests that his ship be withdrawn from class when no survey is overdue and there are no known defects, particulars of the class are removed and a note is inserted in the Supplement. When the Rules as regards surveys on the hull, machinery, or equipment have not been complied with, the class may be withdrawn or suspended by the Committee, and a note to this effect and the date of the decision is made in the Supplement. The class may also be withdrawn when a ship is reported to have serious defects which owners take no steps to repair efficiently and similar action to record this fact is taken.

When a ship sails with less freeboard than that approved, or when the freeboard marks are placed higher than that position assigned by the Committee her class is deleted and expunged from the Register.

In the case of a ship being sunk, wrecked or lost, the class is deleted and a notation as to the cause of the casualty is inserted against the name in the Supplement.

Classification with any other Society is denoted in this column by the initials of the society in question. For example, 'NV' signifies classification with Det. Norske Veritas. If these initials are in parentheses this indicates that the ship formerly held the classification of that Society.

Column (5)

This gives the shipbuilders and yard number, together with date and place of build, dimensions, superstructure, decks, if hull is rivetted/part welded and other details of the hull.

The notation 'NS' (no sparring), also appears in this column against some vessels classed with Lloyd's Register. This term shows that the vessel is not fitted with cargo battens, and therefore the liability for cargo to become damaged by contact with the ship's sides is greater. The point is of interest to shippers and underwriters.

Column (6)

This shows, inter alia, the number of screwshafts (if more than one), the type of propulsion (e.g. steam, motor, diesel electric), and the type of ship (general cargo, tanker, tug, fishing etc.). The maximum number of passengers carried (where applicable) is also recorded; a note if the ship carries refrigerated cargo or containers, whether open or closed shelter deck and the position of the engine room. The number and length of holds, the number of cargo tanks and grain, liquid, bale and insulated capacities are also given, as well as a note of heating coils, fitted in bunker and/or cargo spaces, the number and size of hatches, number of winches and cranes and derricks with their safe working loads.

Column (7)

In this column full particulars are given of the engines and boilers. For the purpose of this volume it is only necessary to draw attention to the notations 'C', 'T', and 'Q' which classify the engines into 'compound', 'triple' or 'quadruple' expansion engines in the case of steamers. The references to oil engines, turbines, steam turbines connected to electric motors and screwshafts (turbo-electric), oil engines connected to motors and screwshafts (diesel-electric) and steam turbines geared to shafts are self explanatory.

Horsepowers for all main engines are recorded and for steam engines the record 'Spt' after the number and description of the main boilers indicates that the boilers are equipped with superheaters.

The capacity of the fuel bunkers is published, when known, followed by an indication of the fuel for which the machinery is fitted. In the case of a steamship the letters (c) coal or (o.f.) oil fuel may be recorded, and for motorships the letters (d.o.) diesel oil or (h.v.f.) high viscosity fuel are used. Details of auxiliary electrical generating plant are included as well as special type of propellers and the service speed of the ship.

Other abbreviations which can appear in this and other columns, but which are not specifically mentioned in these notes, are clearly explained in the Key to the Register.

As regards the principal periodical surveys required for class maintenance, in addition to the Special Surveys already referred to (the requirements for which become progressively more severe as the ship's age increases), the boilers, domestic boilers, screwshafts and steam pipes of a ship are required to be submitted for survey periodically as prescribed by Lloyd's Register Rules which are constantly under review. The main and auxiliary machinery are examined as part of the machinery of Special Survey.

*

There are also published additional volumes:

Statistical Tables, published annually by Lloyd's Register of Shipping contains mid-year analyses of the world merchant fleet of sea-going ships of 100 tons gross or over, excluding sailing ships and non-propelled carft; numbers and tons gross by country of registration, type, size, age, dimensions and draught. Total deadweight tonnages of all ships by country of registration. Also included is a summary table of numbers of ships and tons gross showing the size of principal merchant fleets and world totals since 1909.

Shipbuilding Returns, published quarterly by Lloyd's Register of Shipping, contains analyses of the world order book of sea-going merchant ships of 100 tons gross and over, excluding wood and non-propelled craft (ships under construction and not commenced); numbers of ships and tons gross by country of build, type, propulsion and size. Also included are separate tables showing ships commenced, launched and completed by country of build.

Summary of Merchant Ships Completed, published annually by Lloyd's Register of Shipping, contains output statistics of sea-going merchant ships of 100 tons gross and over, excluding wood and non-propelled craft, completed in the world; numbers of ships and tons gross by country of build, type, size and intended country of registration. There is a separate section for ships launched in the world.

Casualty Return, published by Lloyd's Register of Shipping, is a quarterly summary of sea-going merchant ships of 100 tons gross and over, excluding non-propelled craft, totally lost and ships broken up or otherwise disposed of not consequent upon casualty. It contains brief details of ship, voyage and cargo, circumstances, place and date of loss, and country of disposal. Tables show numbers of ships and tons gross totally lost by casualty category and country of registration and ships broken up etc., by country of registration and place of disposal.

Statistical Summary of Merchant Ships Totally Lost, published annually by Lloyd's Register of Shipping, contains additional cases not included in the quarterly returns together with an index of ships' names appearing in the returns during the year. Annual analyses are given of casualties and demolitions by country of registration, casualty category, type, size, age, and country of disposal. Maps are included showing the geographical distribution of total losses during the year.

□Entries from Lloyd's Register of Ships 1980–81 are shown on pp. 88–9.

Key to the Register of Ships

1	2	3	4	5	6	7
		TONS	CLASSIFICATION	HULL	SHIP TYPE/CARGO FACILITIES	MACHINERY
LR NUMBER Call Sign	SHIPS NAME Former names	Gross Net *Deadwt	Special Survey	Date of build	Shipbuilders – Place of build Yard Number	Propulsion Ship type Shelter deck Passengers	No. & Type of engines Bore × stroke (mm) Design
Official No.	Owners Managers		Hull Machinery	Length overall (m) Breadth extreme (m) Draught maximum (m)	Holds & lengths (m)/Cargo tanks & types	Power Where manufactured
Navigational aids	Flag Port of Registry		Refrigerated cargo installation	B.P. (m) Breadth moulded (m) Depth moulded (m)	Grain/Liquid (m³) Bale Insulated spaces (m³) Heating coils	Enginebuilders Boilers Pressures Heating surface Furnaces
		*(tonnes)	Equipment letter	Superstructures (m) Decks	Containers & lengths (ft)	Aux. electrical generating plant & output
				Rise of floor (mm) Keel moulded (mm)	Hatchways & sizes (m)	Special propellers
				Riveted/Welded Water ballast	Winches Cranes/Derricks (SWL tonnes)	Fuel bunkers (tonnes)
				Bulkheads Alterations Conversions		Speed

REGISTER OF SHIPS 1980-81

HELMUT JUST

7013109 HELMUT JUST — 291 / 156
DHVZ — VEB Bagger-, Bugsier-u. Bergungsreederei — Rostock — German Democratic Republic
DSRK
1952 VEB Schiffswerft "Edgar André"-Magdeburg — 46.00 — 8.06 — 2.699 / 3.00
45.08 — 1 dk
M Hopper Barge — Bottom doors — Mchy.aft
Oil 4SA 6Cy. 240 × 360 — 161kW (216bhp) Schwermasch. Karl Liebknecht — Magdeburg
Gen 1 × 9.5kW 220V 50Hz a.c. — 8kn

6811837 HELMUTH FELDTMANN — T.Mk 499 / 275 / 1 065
DAGG
10795 — Ilse Feldtmann — Hamburg — Federal Republic of Germany
Df Esd Rdr RTm/h/v
Gl
1966 J. J. Sietas Schiffssew.—Hamburg (569) — 61.91 — 10.04 — 4.115
55.02 — 10.01 — 6.20
P 11.0 B 11.9 F 7.7 — 2 dks
rf 76
M General Cargo — 1 Ho 38.4 ER — G 1 999 B 1 832 — 2 Ha (19.2 10.4 × 6.4) ER — 3W Der 3(3)
Oil 4SA 6Cy. 320 × 450 — 373kW (500bhp) Klockner-Humboldt-Deutz — Köln
Gen 2 × 33kW 1 × 19kW — 231/400V a.c. — Fuel 58.0t (d.o.) — 11kn

7014036 HELNES — T.Mk 298 / 90
LLPF
C17475 — Nordkapp Havfiskeselskap A/S — Hammerfest — Norway
Df Esd Gc Rdr RT
NV
1970 Storvika M/V–Kristiansund — 46.54 — 9.00 — 4.560
40.04 — 9.00 — 6.51
2 dks — BK 178
M Stern Trawler Ref (4.1) — Ice strengthened — 1 Ho ER — 1 Ha (2.5 × 1.9) ER
Oil 4SA 8Cy. 320 × 480 — 895kW (1 200bhp) Motorenw. Mannheim — Mannheim
Gen 2 × 68kW 220V 50Hz a.c. — Controllable pitch propeller — Fuel (d.o.)

5147322 HELNY — 498 / 206 / 869
OGAG
1040 — R/A Sally — Algot Johansson — Mariehamn — Finland
Df Rdr RTm
BV
1959 Varv. A. Johansson & Co.–Mariehamn — 67.26 — 9.78 — 3.429
63.00 — 9.76
P 20.2 F 7.7 — 1 dk & S dk
rf 119
M General Cargo (1) — 1 Ho 36.7 ER — G 1 863 B 1 746 — 2 Ha leach 13.1 × 4.5) ER — Cr 2(3)
OSD Oil 4SA 8Cy. 320 × 450 — 791kW (1 060bhp) Klockner-Humboldt-Deutz — Köln
Gen 2 × 52kW 1 × 10.5kW 220V d.c. — Fuel 42.5t (d.o.)+3.5pd — 13kn

6726474 HELOU I — 123 / 58
Df Esd RT — Pakfreeze — Beirut — Lebanon
1967 Ch. Normands Reunis–Courseulles-sur-Mer — 24.80 — 6.81 — 2.286
21.67 — 6.68 — 3.48
1 dk
M Fishing — Side Trawler — 1 Ho — In.141
Oil 4SA 6Cy. 159 × 203 reduction geared — 283kW (380bhp) Caterpillar Tractor Co. — Peoria, Il
Fuel (d.o.) — 9kn

6726486 HELOU II — 123 / 58
Df Esd RT — Pakfreeze — Beirut — Lebanon
1967 Ch. Normands Reunis–Courseulles-sur-Mer — 24.80 — 6.81 — 2.286
21.67 — 6.68 — 3.48
1 dk
M Fishing — Side Trawler — 1 Ho — In.141
Oil 4SA 6Cy. 159 × 203 reduction geared — 283kW (380bhp) Caterpillar Tractor Co. — Peoria, Il
9kn

7413381 HELPFUL HAND
364417 UML Ltd.
Liverpool   United Kingdom
499 / 300 / 965
TM Tank Barge   Michyaft
1975 Yorkshire D.D. Co. Ltd—Hull (237)
40.21   4.420
37.55   9.50   4.73
1 dk
2 Oil 4SA each 6Cy. 140 × 165
272kW (365bhp)
Caterpillar Tractor Co.   Peoria, Il
9kn

5147346 HELSINGOR
OYZX
Government of The Kingdom of Denmark (Danske Statsbaner)
Helsingor   Denmark
Rdr
1123 / 404 / 640
D-E RoRo Cargo/Ferry   Vehicles Rail Vehicles   640dk P
1955 Helsingor Skibsv. og Maskinbyg. (321)
—Helsingor
BV 80.02   12.93   3.582
69.14   12.91   5.26
1 dk
RW rf 305
4 Oil 4SA each 6Cy. 245 × 400 driving 4 gen. each 280kW 220V d.c. connected to 2 elec. motors each of 410kW (550bhp) (CC)
Helsingor Skibsv. og Maskinbyg.   Helsingor
Gen 2 × 280kW, 1 × 170kW 220V d.c.
1 propeller aft 1 fwd
Fuel 42.5t (d.o.)   11kn

6521587 HELTERMAA
UIIV
M-26993 U.S.S.R.-Estonian Shipping Co.
Df Esd Tallin   U.S.S.R.
Gc Rdr
RT
3236 / 1539 / 4234
M General Cargo   "Neptun"—Rostock
Ice strengthened
1964 VEB Schiffswerft "Neptun"—Rostock
RS 105.85   14.64   6.560
95.71   14.53   8.03
2 dks
4 Ho 15.7 15.3 14.4 ER 15.7
G.6248 B.5787
4 Ha (stl) (9.9 9.9 × 7.0) (10.3 × 8.9) ER (10.3 × 8.9)
8W Der 1(35) 4(5) 4(3)
Oil 2SA 6Cy. 570 × 800
2 425kW (3 250bhp)
DMR Dieselmotorenwerk Rostock
Gen 3 × 200kW 380V 50Hz a.c.
Fuel 552.5t (d.o.)   14kn

5147398 HELWAN
SUIK
43 The Egyptian Navigation Co.
Df Esd Alexandria   Egypt
Gc Rdr
RT
1946 / 1250 / 2941
M General Cargo
1980 VEB Schiffswerft "Neptun"—Rostock
85.20   12.07   5.716
12.02   6.81
GL P 15.6 F 8.3 2 dks
CSD Oil 4SA 6Cy. 420 × 660
1 231kW (1 650bhp)
Klockner-Humboldt-Deutz   Koln

7628798 HELWAN
341 Qatar National Navigation & Transport Co. Ltd.
Rdr Doha   Qatar
56 ✠100A1
34 tug
Arabian Gulf service west of a line Bandar Abbas to Ras al Khaimah
✠LMC
EL (B) ⌷U2 4BH W8BT
TM Tug
1977-2 Sing Koon Seng Shipyard (393 T)
—Singapore
17.20   5.87   2.306
16.21   5.69   2.67
1 dk
rf 787
2 Oil 4SA each 6Cy. 137 × 165 reverse reduction geared to 2 sc. shafts
Caterpillar Tractor Co.   Peoria, Il
Gen 2 × 10kW 440V 50Hz a.c.

7802201 HEMANTSAGAR
ATRS
Shaparia Shipping & Allied Industries Pvt. Ltd.
RT Bombay   India
492 / 305 / 688
TM General Cargo
1977 Shaparia Dock & Steel Co. Ltd. (Z174)
—Bombay
BV 51.52   9.94   2.401
49.59   9.50   3.05
1 dk
rf nil
1 Ho 31.8 ER
G.662
1 Ha (w) (26.8 × 6.4) ER
10W
2 Oil 4SA each 8Cy. 175 × 220 reduction geared
380kW (510bhp)
Kirloskar Oil Engines Ltd.
Gen 1 × 12.5kW 1 × 10kW 415V 50Hz a.c.
Fuel 9.0t (d.o.)-2.5pd   9kn

5289566 HEMERICA
TOQP ex Pactole-71
4119 Societe Anonyme Armement Nicot
Df Esd Concarneau   France
Pfd Rdr
RT
202 / 70 / —
M Fishing   Side Trawler
1958 At. & Forg. de l'Ouest—St. Nazaire (Ch17)
BV 34.80   6.96   3.601
30.00   6.90   4.35
1 dk
RW
5 Ha (1.0 × 8.6) (1.0 × 8.3) (0.9 0.9 × 0.9) (0.6 × 0.5)
Der 1(1)
Oil 4SA 6Cy. 315 × 480
448kW (600bhp)
Moteurs Duvant
Fuel 56.0t (d.o.)
Valenciennes   12kn

7611781 HEMINA
LGCN
19070 K/S A/S Heroges
Df Esd Helge R. Myhre
Gc Pfd Stavanger   Norway
Rdr RT
1999 / 1011 / 3058
M Liquefied Gas Carrier   LPG
1977 Moss Rosenberg Verft A/S—Moss (189)
NV 75.72 (BB)   14.03   5.501
70.11   14.01   7.90
P. F.   1 dk
Ice strengthened 2 Ta (stl) ind
1 double-cyl conical horizontal
1 double-cyl horizontal
Methan/1
L.2 450 L.(gas) 2 450
Oil 2SA 9Cy. 300 × 450
2 238kW (3 000bhp)
Wichmann Motorfabrik
Gen 4 × 215kW
Controllable pitch propeller
Thw. thrust propeller fwd
Rubbestadneset   13kn

16 Ownership, Sale and Purchase of Vessels

The persons who are entitled to own a British ship are British born subjects carrying on business in British countries, naturalized subjects who carry out their business in British countries, and corporate bodies whose principal place of business is the United Kingdom or a British Dominion.

A British ship is a vessel flying the British flag, and in passing, a brief outline of the 'Law of the Flag' may assist the reader. Under the law of the flag a vessel becomes subject to the country whose flag she is flying, and the conduct of the affairs on board is governed by the laws of that country. When, however, a vessel enters the waters of a foreign power she is bound to conform to the laws of the country in whose waters she is.

The members of the crew are subject to the laws of the country under whose flag the ship is sailing, and are not in any way controlled by the laws of the country of which they are subjects.

The ownership of a British vessel is divided by ancient custom into sixty-fourths, a division which is recognized in law by its inclusion in Sect. 5 of the Merchant Shipping Act 1894.

A vessel may not be registered in more than 64 names, and where a limited company is an owner it is registered under its corporate name and not the names of its individual shareholders.

All ships must be registered, excluding small vessels of under fifteen tons burden employed in river or coastal trade, or ships under thirty tons burden employed for fishing or trading on the shores of Newfoundland. An unregistered ship carries unlimited liability.

Before being registered every ship must have its name marked upon the bows, its name and port of registry on the stern, and the official number of the ship and registered tonnage cut in the main beam of the ship in a permanent manner. In the case of wood vessels this is burnt into the beam, whilst with steel ships these particulars are punched in the beam.

Where the main beam is not accessible, the number is cut into the forward hatch coaming.

Upon the stem and stern post a scale of feet denoting the draught of the vessel must be marked.

In the case of new vessels the ship must be surveyed, and a certificate of survey produced giving full identification of the vessel, together with a builder's certificate giving particulars of the ship and the persons entitled to be registered as owners.

The owner then gives a declaration of his right to become an owner and his qualification, place of building of the ship, the name of the master, and a statement that no unqualified person is holding a share in the ship. A company or corporate body makes this declaration through its secretary by document under seal.

At the same time the ship's husband or ship's managing owner is registered. He is the person who accepts individual liability for the obligations of the owner and is personally answerable to the Courts.

Registration of the ship is made at the port by the Principal Officer of Customs, who enters into the register book the name of the ship and port of registry, details of the ship and particulars of ownership. The registrar retains the surveyor's certificate, carving note, builder's certificate, and bill of sale. The registrar then issues a *Certificate of Registry* (known as the *ship's register*), which is only a document of registration for use in the navigation of the ship.

Change of ownership, or change of master, must be endorsed upon the ship's register, and in the event of the ship becoming lost, taken by an enemy, or ceasing to be a British vessel, the certificate of registry must be given up. At any time when change of ownership of a vessel occurs, a bill of sale is made out even if no money passes. The Bill of Sale Act 1882 *does not apply to the sale of ships*. The bill of sale and declaration of transfer is produced to the registrar, who records the particulars of this transaction in the register book, and endorses the certificate of registry accordingly. A ship sale *agreement* does not require to be executed under seal, nor does it or any other document concerning a ship sale require stamping in the United Kingdom. A *Bill of Sale* (of a ship) must be under Seal.

It is usual when a ship is sold for the vessel to be dry docked for hull inspection, and if after such an inspection the report is not favourable, or the purchaser is not satisfied, the expenses of such a survey are for account of the vendor. Should, however, the survey prove satisfactory then a deposit usually of 10 per cent is made, and the balance of purchase money paid over on completion.

On sale or loss of the ship, the official log is returned to the superintendent at Port of Registry.

When signing articles, the crew make the contract with the master as agent for the owners, and such contract must be considered apart from ownership of the vessel. If the ownership changes, the original owner ceasing to run his vessel, then the terms of employment are changed and the crew may claim immediate repatriation. See also notes in chapter 12. The crew have the option upon the transfer of ownership of a vessel of requesting their discharge with full repatriation, or of signing fresh articles with the new owners.

In the majority of cases the crews are agreeable to sign fresh articles, but owners have no control over this action, and must if the men desire arrange for their return by repatriation.

17 Ship's Papers and Procedure of Ship's Entering and Leaving Port

A ship must carry the following papers, and the master must, if required, produce them to any Customs Officers, Department of Trade officers, Mercantile Marine Superintendent, officer of H.M. Navy, or consul —

- (a) Maritime Declaration of Health and current De-Ratisation Certificate.
- (b) Certificate of registry (or ship's register).
- (c) Ship's articles.
- (d) Manifest.
- (e) Charter-party or bills of lading.
- (f) Official log.
- (g) List of dutiable stores (not available unless in port).
- (h) Loadline Certificate.
- (i) Wireless Installation Inspection Certificate.

The *Maritime Declaration of Health* is a certificate which states that the health of the vessel or every person on board is in good condition, free from contagious diseases, there being no reason why the vessel should not enter the port. The master can obtain this certificate by radio from the Port Health Officer in London when the vessel is coming from certain listed ports, e.g. those within Europe and North America. (Other UK ports may adopt this procedure.) The master gives a period of time of notice of arrival at a UK port, declaring the health of all on board is satisfactory and 'Free Practique' will be granted by the port Health Authorities on arrival. Or, it may certify that the port from which the ship has arrived was 'clean' and free from disease when the vessel left.

The *De-Ratisation Certificate*, which normally lasts 6 months, certifies that the ship has been dealt with by an approved authority to free the ships of rats.

The Certificate of Registry has been referred to in a previous chapter. This document must always be carried on board.

The *ship's articles* contain a description of the crew and the capacity in which each member serves, length of voyage, amount of wages, time of commencement of voyage, and scale of provisions. This is the agreement between the master and his crew, and must be referred to when signing on or signing off the crew.

The *manifest* is the list of cargo on board the ship, and gives the full particulars of contents, marks, shippers and receivers. This is often described as an 'inventory' of all cargo on board.

Whilst charter-parties or bills of lading, under which the cargo is being carried are included in this list it should be remembered that in many cases vessels leave a port without the manifest or bills of lading on board. It is often found convenient to send these papers to the port of destination of the ship by a following vessel, which arrives earlier, or by air mail. This procedure gives the shipping office (at port of loading) additional time for the preparation of documents, and the documents are received at port of destination some few days prior to the vessel's arrival, providing a saving of time at both ports. As the manifest or bills of lading are only required at port of destination no objections are raised if the vessel does not carry such documents provided they are received at port of discharge before or at time of arrival of the ship.

Official logs must be kept on every ship in the approved form of the Department of Trade. All entries made in these books must be made as soon as possible after an occurrence, and signed by the master and mate, or other member of the crew. Entries referring to illness must be signed by the ship's surgeon (if one is employed on board); entries regarding wages must be signed by the master, mate, and some member of the crew.

All entries in official log books are admissible as evidence in any proceedings in a court of justice.

Entries in the official log book consist of all records of crew's conduct, wages, fines, any births, marriages, or deaths. Happenings in regard to the procedure of the ship are entered on the ship's log.

A list of dutiable stores is carried on board for customs purposes. This is made up by a Ship's Officer and checked by the Customs Officer on boarding the ship.

On arrival at the port of destination, the master presents the Maritime Declaration of Health to the medical officer of the port, who after satisfying himself that there is no objection to the ship—on the ground of health—passes it in as 'clean'.

The Rummaging Officer or Customs Preventative Officer comes on board and compares the list of stores with the amount in the ship's various store rooms. If in agreement, the dutiable stores are sealed and remain so sealed whilst in port. He then searches the ship, seeking contraband as a preventive measure against smuggling.

The master applies to the pilot to bring the ship to the dock or berth.

In order to cope with the extremely fast turnround of some modern ships and to streamline certain procedures the Customs authorities issued in January 1978, Customs Notice No. 69, effective on 1 April 1978. This gives notice of changes in procedure and documentation and additional responsibilities of Masters, agents and ships' suppliers arising from a selective boarding system for commercial vessels with new forms. There will also be changes for shipping and controlling duty-free stores.

When a vessel is not boarded on arrival a Master or his authorized agent is required to lodge all boarding documents at a Customs office as designated.

The notice gives details of the revised procedure and sets out the additional responsibilities of Masters and agents. Their existing legal responsibilities are not affected.

The forms are given:

Form C.13   General Declaration.
Form C.14   Ship's Stores Declaration.
Form C.142   Crew Declaration.
Form C.143   Small Parcel List   ⎫ If
Form D.C.I. Self-declaration Deck Cargo ⎬ appropriate

(Form D.C.I. is a new form covering cargo on deck and in unregistered spaces as well as oil fuel in double-bottoms or other ballast tanks.)

If a vessel is not boarded on arrival, one copy of each form must be lodged at the designated Customs office by the Master or agent within 3 hours of arrival. Collectors will have discretion to adjust this period in special circumstances.

Other complementary requirements are also specified, and a study of the requirements of this Notice No.69 is recommended.

Report and clearance of vessels will continue as at present.

If the ship is in ballast and coming inwards a Custom House Report is needed. If the ship is with cargo, there is, in addition, the report and list of dutiable stores; also—

(1) Register   (4) Tonnage slip
(2) Stores list   (5) Pilotage slip
(3) Lights certificate

Every ship must produce a light dues receipt either before entering or before leaving the port. No ship is allowed to leave port without the light dues being paid.

Light dues are payable at a fee which fluctuates so much per ton, and the money received from this levy assists in the maintenance of all lights, lightships, lighthouses, beacons, etc., around the coast. The lights which are maintained by the Corporation of Trinity House (although the levies are often collected through local port authorities) out of the levies include the Great Basses, Little Basses, and Minnecoy Lights.

The Bahamas Lights, however, are maintained from money voted by Parliament for this specific purpose.

Every ship, whether laden or in ballast, must report after arrival from any port abroad, or any port in the United Kingdom.

Vessels from foreign ports which put into British ports purely for bunker purposes, provisions, or as a port of refuge, are not required to report unless the vessel remains in port for more than 24 hours from the time of arrival.

Failure on the part of a master to report his ship makes him personally liable for a fine of £100, and all goods which are not reported may be detained.

When a ship arrives or is expected to arrive out of legal hours for reporting, the Collector of Customs may on receiving a request in writing, allow bulk to be broken, prior to report being lodged. This permission, however, does not relieve the ship from its responsibility of reporting within the stipulated period of 24 hours.

In the case of a vessel sailing outwards, the procedure is reversed. The master must obtain a shipping bill for stores, and present to the Custom House a report of the cargo he is carrying outwards within six days.

He must also produce the light dues receipt, and his clean Maritime Declaration of Health before the clearance is obtained.

The master must appear in person or alternatively appoint an agent, by signing Customs Form C74 to make report or clear the vessel.

The documents required for *Clearance* are—

Register

Load line certificate

Safety Radio/Telegraphy
    certificate

Safety Equipment certificate

Cargo Ship Safety Construction
    certificate

Light bill

Pilotage receipt (for
    foreign owned vessels only)

Application is then made to the pilot to see the ship clear from the waters of the port.

18 Voyage Estimates

This chapter is not intended to deal with the operation of accountancy in relation to the records kept for every voyage that a ship may make, but only to make reference to the estimating for fixing purposes.

In the case of ordinary liner berth shipments, where a vessel loads whatever cargo may be offered to her, at the rates which are agreed by the various Conferences, there is less necessity for an estimated voyage account.

When an owner has an opportunity to quote for a fixture, he must know what figure he is to offer the broker in order to secure a profit, and an estimation of his proposed earnings and expenses is made.

The estimated expenses are ascertained, and the division of this amount by the number of tons of cargo to be carried results in the cost per ton of transportation. To this amount is added the profit desired, and the rate of freight for quotation purposes is found.

If the state of the market is calling for a higher rate, then his percentage of profits is increased. If, however, rates are low, then he knows at what rate he may or must quote in order to clear his expenses and also avoid a loss.

It is sometimes to the advantage of an owner in times of depression to secure a cargo at a rate which will produce a small loss, for although out of pocket to the extent of his financial loss he has retained a hold of trade, and does not incur expense in laying up his vessel. Charges for laying up are variable, and an owner who wishes to lay a ship up for a period of time naturally finds accommodation at the cheapest places.

A vessel laid up tends to deteriorate at a far quicker rate than when it is actually operating.

It is occasionally found that in times of bad trade a new vessel is built and immediately laid up. This is accounted for by the fact that during times of depression building rates tend to be lower than in times of boom, and enterprising owners quick to take advantage of a reduction in building costs give orders for new vessels at fixed costs to replace old ones which they may sell, and thus, following the axiom that boom follows depression, are equipped with a new vessel in readiness for the time when the return of trade is evident.

Whilst dealing with this point it may be observed that the very controversial matter of scrapping or selling vessels when they are replaced has been the topic from time to time of many discussions in the shipping world. An owner when he disposes of old tonnage has the alternative of having it sold as scrap for a reduced sum or receiving a considerably higher figure by sale to foreign owners. This increase of income is offset in the United Kingdom by taxation and the fact that the new foreign owner is often quick to use his newly acquired vessel in opposition to the very owner from whom he purchased her. If, however, a British owner provides sufficiently for depreciation in his accounts, there is no reason why, when a vessel is to be disposed of, she should not secure more than her book value in the money paid for her as scrap. By this method the shareholders of the owning company are at no disadvantage, and the possibility of competition by their old vessels is avoided.

To return however, to the estimation of running costs the main items are fuel, daily running expenses and port charges.

The first point is to ascertain how long the vessel will be on her trip. This is arrived at by dividing the total distance by the distance the ship will travel each day, thus finding the number of days the vessel will be on voyage, plus the time spent in port.

If a ship is a 10 knot steamer then she should obviously cover 240 miles per day, but actually a coal fired steam ship never runs to the total of this amount, and it is safer to assume that the nearer estimate would be to multiply the number of knots by 22 rather than by 24 (hours per day). Therefore, estimated travelling capacity of a 10 knot steamer would be approximately 215–225 miles per day but an oil fired steam ship, or a motor vessel should maintain 240 m.p.d. subject to weather.

A third point that has to be considered is the question of expenses in connection with time spent in port, and port charges and cargo charges.

It is as well to remember that the main *port charge* is usually either dock dues, river dues or harbour dues, according to the port visited, and in most ports of the world such dues are usually based on the net registered tonnage (N.R.T.) of the vessel, that is to say, so much per N.R.T.

In UK ports the vessel will have to pay *light dues* also based on N.R.T. and at a great number of ports *pilotage*, and possibly *towage charges* will be incurred, and usually an agency fee must be allowed for.

Under *cargo charges* will come stevedores' charges for loading or discharging, dunnage and separation, also tallying, but whether these appear on the estimate will depend upon the terms of the C/P, which may provide for free loading and/or discharging.

Commissions payable must also be calculated in the estimate.

From known particulars a simplified estimated account may be drawn up (Note: one-way voyage) and would read as follows:

No: . . . .

VOYAGE ESTIMATE . . . .   Date . . . . 19 . . . .

s.s./m.v. ". . . . ."   N.R.T. . . . . D.W. Total . . . . 15,000 tons

Less: Stores   350 tons

Bkrs. HVF. 425 tons

D.O.   60 tons   835 tons

Cargo — Grain in Bulk.

(F.I.O. terms)   Total D.W.C.C. . . . . 14,165 tons

---

From: New Orleans   To: Liverpool. (Seaforth Dk.)

4735 miles @ 14.5 knots (allow reduced speed in approaches) = 14 days

---

Freight: 14,165 tons @ $23.00 = $325,795.00 $314,392.18   £

F.I.O.:   Less commission @ 3½% = $11,402.82   146,228

Days at Sea	Days in Port	Disbursements			
14	3	Load: New Orleans $11,900 = £ 5534			
	4	Discharge: Liverpool £18,000	£23,534		
Total days 21.		Bkrs— 14 days @ 25 t.p.d.			
		plus 3 days, 425 tons			
		HVF @ $180 p.t. = $76,500 = £35,581			
(Plus Bunker Safety margin 3 days.)		D.O. @ 2.5 t.p.d. 21 days			
		plus 3 days = 60 tons			
		@ $350 p.t. = $21,000 = £ 9,767	£45,348		
		D.R.C. £2,500 x 21 days	£52,500	121,382	

Currency conversion $2.15 = £1.   Profit   £24,846

Profit per day   £ 1,183

The division of the speed into the total mileage gives the estimated voyage time occupied. If, for example, the vessel, a motor vessel, is to proceed from Swansea to Rio de Janeiro, 5010 miles at 10 knots, the time occupied would amount to 21 days. But with a notional margin of say two days allowance for possible adverse weather, it may be better to estimate 23 days.

Secondly, the ship has to be provided with bunkers for the proposed trip, assuming she will re-bunker at port of destination. This latter point is a matter which must be checked with the bunker suppliers to verify that adequate stocks of appropriate fuels are held at the place concerned.

The amount of fuel used per day differs according to the type of ship, the engine power, and consequently, her speed. In calculations for voyage cost estimates, the particular ship's daily consumption will be known, and it is always prudent to allow for possible delays due to stress of weather or other unforeseeable circumstances causing the ship to be longer on the trip than the simple 'miles per day into the total distance', as mentioned in an earlier paragraph. Also allowance must be made for time in port and for bunkers used whilst the ship is in port.

The daily running costs of a ship — D.R.C. — are fundamentally dependent upon which items of cost any given owner includes is his assessment. For instance, some owners include an estimated figure to cover depreciation.

But if reduced to relatively straightforward items such as Food, Wages, Insurance and Stores, plus an allocation towards the cost of periodic maintenance and repair costs, and allowing for Management charges, etc., these several items would total—on a S.D.14 type of ship at 1980 costs—about £2500 per day.

It will be readily appreciated that the foregoing charges may vary considerably from ship to ship, according to net registered tonnage, the value for which she is insured, the number of crew carried, etc.

Whichever basis be selected by individual owners, they will know what margins their calculations include, and can therefore judge whether specific business which they may be contemplating is economically viable or whether further consideration, such as the value of positioning the ship for subsequent business must be taken into account.

No two vessels can be assessed at the same figure, as there are always some variations which defeat such 'grouping' calculations.

It must be remembered that the above estimate is merely by way of illustration and cannot be taken as of actual detailed charges.

Allowances must also be made where under particular charter-party terms additional commissions are allowable, and consideration must also be given to individual ports—as to whether loading is fast or slow, any extra time or expenses incurred, also the charges for stevedoring and port charges which again vary in every locality, and whether and to what extent dispatch or demurrage is payable.

Another point which must be considered is the fact that if a vessel is able to carry out her voyage by alternative routes then estimates of such alternatives must be made. For example, a vessel from South Wales to Australian ports would have the option of proceeding via Cape Town, or via Suez or Panama, in which case the consideration of extra distance via Cape Town (a matter of about 1200 miles) would be neutralized by the expenses saved in avoiding the tolls of the canals.

The possibility of dividing the trip into stages for the purpose of obtaining bunkers is another consideration. If, for example, a vessel is able to call at two intermediate ports for bunker purposes on route then the space or weight allowed for bunkers would automatically be less, and thus if desirable used for cargo purposes. The greater the amount of bunkers loaded on board at the commencement of the voyage the less cargo space or deadweight available, and in many cases where estimates are drawn up for a voyage this point would provide an increased earning capacity for the vessel. Against the increased freight earned, there would have to be offset such additional expenses, if any, of increased cost of bunker charges, and the cost of time and of entering and leaving the chosen bunker port.

The consideration of a voyage being split into bunkering stages was very important in the case of coal burning steam ships owing to the large quantities of coal consumed, and therefore its weight relative to the total deadweight of the ship concerned. Oil firing, or the more modest daily consumption of diesel engines, permits of less frequent bunker calls. Another factor which enters into the matter nowadays is the relatively high daily running cost of almost any ship, making every day saved an important contribution to operating success.

When a vessel has completed her discharge, the owner, if he has no other engagement in view, or if desirous of returning the ship to her port of loading in ballast, should add such cost of return to the original figures.

It is unnecessary to add that in the example the vessel is assumed to be in position at loading port and if this were not so due allowance would have to be made for time and expense of proceeding there from the previous discharging port.

The assessment of the business would still not be complete unless due consideration had been given to further employment on completion of discharge.

19 Distances

The nautical mile varies from 6045.93 ft. on the equator to 6107.98 ft. in lat. 90°, and the length of a mean nautical mile is 6076 ft., whilst the Admiralty measured mile is 6080 ft.

A *knot* is one nautical mile per hour, and is a measure of speed. A vessel whose speed is 10 knots, covers 10 nautical miles per hour, but the knot is frequently used, although wrongly, to denote a nautical mile.

The following table of distances in nautical miles should be memorized where possible. The inclusion of a greater number of distances in this volume is not possible owing to limitation of space.

DISTANCES FROM LONDON

Belfast	660	Liverpool	640
Bristol	520	Manchester	680
Cardiff	500	Newcastle	300
Dundee	400	Newport	510
Glasgow	750	Southampton	190
Hull	210	Swansea	480
Ipswich	75		
Aarhus	570	Klaipeda	825
Arkhangel'sk	2060	Narvik	1230
Turku	995	Pitea	1250
Copenhagen	580	Tallinn	1020
Gdansk	790	Riga	995
Gärle	1010	Skaw	550
Gothenburg	590	Szczecin	630
Kiel	436	Stockholm	900
Liepaja	850	Tornio	1300
Lulea	1260		
Amsterdam	185	Hamburg	410
Antwerp	175	Havre	190
Bilbao	720	Lisbon	1030
Bordeaux	673	Nantes	570
Bremen	375	Rotterdam	160
Brest	408	Rouen	255
Dunkirk	95	Santander	690
Gibraltar	1300	Vigo	800

Alexandria	3100	Naples	2280
Algiers	1720	Piraeus	2820
Barcelona	1840	Port Said	3220
Fiume (Rijeka)	2960	Sfax	2260
Leghorn	2170	Toulon	2000
Malta	2290	Tunis	2085
Marseilles	2000		

Aden	4620	Karachi	6090
Beira	7265	Mauritius	6960
Bombay	6290	Mozambique	6770
Calcutta	7970	Penang	7990
Colombo	6710	Rangoon	7980
Dar-es-Salaam	6360	Singapore	8280
Djakarta (Jakarta)	8520	Zanzibar	6380

Hsiamen	9970	Nagasaki	10,730
Canton	9750	Saigon	8900
Hong Kong	9720	Shanghai	10,520
Kobe	11,010	Wei-hai	10,840
Manila	9670	Yokohama	11,235
Ujung Pangdang	9270		

Adelaide	10,720	Melbourne	11,020
Auckland	12,670	Newcastle, N.S.W.	11,550
Brisbane	11,890	Sydney	11,490
Fremantle	9520	Wellington	12,420

Accra	3950	Lagos	4240
Durban	6990	Mossel Bay	6390
Bathurst	2630	Natal	6990
Cape Town	6150	Sierra Leone	3010
East London	6710	Walvis Bay	5530
Inhambane	7440		

Ascension	3900	Madeira	1460
Las Palmas	1680	Teneriffe	1677

Bahia	4500	Magallanes	7450
Bahia Blanca	6550	Montevideo	6210
Buenos Aires	6330	Para	4130
Cape Horn	7550	Rio de Janeiro	5200
Demerara (Georgetown)	4040	Santos	5380

Antigua	3630	Havana	4310
Barbados	3750	St. Lucia	3760
Bermuda	3040	San Domingo	3970
Colon	4720	Santiago	4150

Baltimore	3500	Newport	3370
Boston	3000	New York	3200
Galveston	5000	Philadelphia	2980
Montreal	3140	St. John, N.B.	2910
New Orleans	4810	St. John's, N.F.	2150
Antofogasta	6900	San Diego	7735
Iquiqui	6770	Valparaiso	7380
Mollendo	6550		

CROSS DISTANCES

Auckland	to Dunedin	830
Auckland	to San Francisco	5500
Azores	to Melbourne	11,800
Baltimore	to Algoa Bay	7330
Bombay	to Calcutta	2150
Brisbane	to Darwin	2000
Brisbane	to New York	9840
Calcutta	to Sydney, N.S.W.	6150
Cape Town	to Colombo	4350
Cape Town	to Melbourne	5900
Cape Town	to Singapore	5715
Durban	to Adelaide	5220
Gibraltar	to Beirut	2004
Gibraltar	to Key West	4050
Havre	to Gdansk	900
Hong Kong	to Adelaide	4700
Hong Kong	to Manila	625
Hong Kong	to San Francisco	6090
Kingston (Ja.)	to Colon	545
La Guiara	to Colon	725
La Guiara	to Kingston (Ja.)	725
Lisbon	to Seville	290
Madeira	to Wellington	10,290
Mollendo	to Panama	1770
New York	to Buenos Aires	5910
New York	to Cape Town	6800
New York	to Gibraltar	3145
New York	to Port of Spain	1930
Panama	to Sydney, N.S.W.	8000
Panama	to Yokohama	8000
Port of Spain	to New Orleans	2052
Port Said	to Aden	1400
Philadelphia	to Shanghai	10,480
Rio de Janeiro	to Cape Town	3275

Rio de Janeiro . . . . to Gibraltar 4235
Rotterdam . . . . to Kiel 370
Shanghai . . . . to Wei-hai 500
Singapore . . . . to Hong Kong 1435
Sydney, N.S.W. . . . . to Fremantle 2100
Sydney, N.S.W. . . . . to Melbourne.. 575
Sydney, N.S.W. . . . . to Wellington 1240
Szczecin . . . . to Tornio 790
Tallinn . . . . to Swansea 1420
Ushant . . . . to Rotterdam 450

20 Containerization

Historians will go back to 1066 and beyond, even to Noah's Ark, to counter claims that the roll-on, roll-off ferry was an immediate post-war concept, brought about by the success of tank landing craft. By the same token, many will argue that the word containerization that has recently crept into our language—and grated on so many ears—is nothing more than cargo carried in big boxes, in much the same way as it has been for hundreds of years. Certainly, the British and Continental Railways were using small, standard sized containers on their services to the Continent and Ireland just prior to World War I and more extensively during the '30s. The Americans used containers of a kind in military transports during World War II and increasingly in their home waters and coastal traffic since then.

But the form of containerization as we know it today and which is now commonplace on the short sea and ferry routes and has penetrated into the deep sea liner trades is a system of handling general cargo by highly mechanized, intermodal methods. The containers are usually 20 ft (6.1 m) or 40 ft (12.2 m) long, 8 ft (2.4 m) wide but of varying heights. In 1982 their construction and minimum maintenance standards will be governed by the Container Safety Convention to which a majority of Governments has acceded and which requires bi-annual inspection and re-certification of every container.

Containers are built of a variety of materials: generally they have steel or aluminium frames with panels being of steel, aluminium, plywood or GRP. At each corner is an external lifting/securing point to an internationally standardized design which permits the containers to be lifted by machinery generally using mechanically operated 'twist locks' which, as their name implies, enter the corner fittings, turn through 90° and so 'lock' the container to the lifting or securing device. The choice of construction materials usually reflects the owner's assessment of initial cost and the subsequent maintenance effort required but weight can be an important feature in trades where the cargo is heavy in relation to its volume. Most countries have a legal or practical limitation to the gross weight of the loaded container and naturally there is an incentive for container operators to keep the tare weight of containers low so as to avoid being restricted by cargo weight rather than by its volume.

There is a considerable variety in the style of containers. Initially they were basically straightforward large and re-useable boxes with doors at one end and of a construction which was internationally acceptable to Customs for crossing borders under Customs seal. However, as the benefits of the system became apparent so there was demand for purpose-built containers—refrigerated, insulated, tanks for liquids of all sorts, bulk powders and grains, liquified gases, items requiring loading from the top or the sides and so on. Some of these 'specials' are not weatherproof but this frequently coincides with cargoes that do not require such protection. Other 'specials' require particular facilities on shore and on ship such as electricity supply for running refrigeration machinery or connection to blown cold air units. The common feature to all is compatibility with fast and highly mechanized handling which brings to the amorphous general cargo carriage many of the benefits of bulk carriage methods.

The container system is capital intensive. It requires large investment in shore installations for holding, filling and emptying containers, operations which may be undertaken in a country's hinterland either by a generally available Container Freight Station in which individually small consignments are made up into container loads, or by a manufacturer or warehouseman whose volume of traffic is sufficiently large to fill containers on his own account. The system needs specially adapted railway trains and road vehicles which can be used intensively and loaded or discharged quickly without the actual goods being handled in the process. Thus the railheads and road interchange points also require automated lifting equipment. Special berths are needed at the ports to hold thousands of containers in transit and equipped to load and discharge the specially designed container ships in a minimum of time. The ships themselves are generally much larger than the cargo liners they have replaced, thus further reaping benefits of scale. Arising from the fast turnround of the ships— and this has frequently been amplified by a reduction in the number of ports of call using land facilities or small 'feeder' vessels to collect and distribute the containers over a large catchment area—the mainstream container ships are able to spend far more of their life at sea. As one operator put it, 'we sell containers in motion, every time they stop moving they cost us money.'

The heavy capital cost of establishing a container system can only be justified by strictly reducing the number of times individual pieces of cargo are handled (ideally twice, once into the container at origin and once out of it at destination) and by intensive use of the equipment. This has led to vertical integration within deep sea transport and to a lesser extent over the shorter routes. Long established liner shipping companies found it necessary to control the overall operation in order to achieve the required intensity and thus they established or bought into port terminals, inland transport companies, container freight stations and so on, thereby establishing a controlled through transport system in which the owner of the goods need deal with only one operator to have his cargo moved from, for example, the factory in Europe to a departmental store in Australia.

In addition to vertical integration, the development of large container ships (some capable of carrying 2800 twenty-foot containers) resulted in rationalization of services between competing shipping companies. The character of deep sea liner shipping in particular has been radically altered. We have seen the amalgamation of companies into a new, single, container operating company, e.g. Overseas Containers Limited, whose shareholders previously operated individually and often in competition with each other. We have also seen the formation of operating consortia whose members each supply ships which are scheduled as a single fleet but whose capacity is shared between the members. Both of these developments arose naturally as a solution to the conflict of 'large is beautiful' with the need for frequency of service.

While containerization cannot be applied to all general cargo and requirements will continue to exist for conventional vessels, for Ro-Ro ships and for other specialized transport, it cannot be denied that the system has proved beneficial to cargo owners and to the shipowners/ container operators. The traders have been supplied with a faster and more secure form of international transport—less packaging, less loss, simplified transport, improved reliability and stability. The shipowners turned container operators have been able to improve their return on investment and to hold down cost increases to a degree that would not otherwise have been possible. Environmentally, the container system offers advantages, as much long-distance land transport can economically be effected by rail. While various bodies lobby against the 'juggernaut' container lorry, one large lorry should replace two or three smaller ones which—given sensible guidance—should mean less public nuisance overall. Such a dramatic change in cargo carrying methods in a relatively short time scale (15 years) could not escape creating social and human problems. Much has been achieved towards coming to terms with the container system and inevitably compromises have been necessary. However, the system is here to stay and doubtless sensibly argued environmental, labour and economic pressures will bring about its overall acceptance.

Documents for Containerized Cargo

With regard to documentation and procedure, the companies concerned operate their own differing arrangements, making it necessary for shippers to ascertain the particular requirements of each carrier. A standard bill of lading is in force in many conferences (see p. 27).

The basic principles set out in earlier chapters relating to sea carriage of goods are not varied.

Where a ship owner accepts goods in containers as part of a general cargo, no problems arise as these are treated as normal cargo, bills being issued in the ordinary way. Here the shipper is merely using the container as a more advantageous method of packing.

When a shipper uses the services of a fully containerized vessel, he is involved in an operation which not only provides sea carriage, but also transportation prior to loading, and again after delivery. Consequently he is concerned with a combined transport bill of lading, which in purpose is not unlike a 'through' bill used ordinarily.

A point of importance is that the container bill is for the acceptance of goods at a prior place, and time, with the intention to load, carry and deliver at a subsequent date. Whilst the sea carriage comes within the Carriage of Goods by Sea Act, the conditions relating to the rest of the operation are set out in the documents and should be examined.

In some cases the shipper carries out his own documentation, and in others he provides the details to the carrier who makes out the bill.

If the carrier accepts full containers the shipper will receive a bill for the total number of containers and details of their contents.

When the goods are sent to an assembly depot and packed with other goods, then the bill acknowledges the number of packages and/or pieces and details their contents.

Because of the nature of containerized vessels, containers carried on deck are carried within the normal course, and whilst liable for General Average if any, must come within the accepted responsibilities and exceptions clauses of carriage.

Terms of letters of credit will have to be varied to meet the difference between an 'acceptance' bill and a 'shipped' bill, but with the increased awareness of banks to changing circumstances this problem can be met and overcome.

There are many related interests to be watched, as for example insurance risks, for whilst the risk of theft and pilferage at docks and during a voyage are reduced, this risk certainly increases on land.

21 Cargoes, Stowage of Cargo, and Cargo Information

The shipowner is responsible for improper or bad stowage, and he is not relieved from liability for any loss occasioned by this no matter how many clauses he may insert in his bills of lading or charter-parties with that object.

The master has control and is directly responsible for the safe handling, loading, stowage, and carriage, care and custody of the goods, and it is one of his primary duties to see that neither the ship nor the cargo is damaged. He is considered to be a competent stevedore and have a full knowledge of safe stowage.

The order of shipment is arranged by the master, and several points must be borne in mind. First, cargo is stowed in the ship in the reverse order to that in which the goods are to be taken out, for example, a ship calling at three ports, namely, A, B, and C, consecutively, must load its cargo in the order of C, B, and A, cargo for Port C first, and Cargo for Port A last, the master bearing in mind, whilst the loading is in operation, that when the cargo for Port A is removed, the ship is still partly loaded, and the cargo remaining on board must be in such a position that it does not have to be rearranged before the vessel may safely proceed to port B. The same conditions apply at Port B, when the cargo on board for Port C is the only cargo remaining stowed.

A competent stevedore would in his loading operations see that heavy cargoes were not stowed over light cargoes, and it is the master's responsibility to see that the stevedore properly carries out his duties in this respect. Also types of cargo which would be liable to cause damage to other cargo should be separated in an efficient manner as a preventive of possible cargo claims.

Any cargo which may be found damaged when loading is commenced should be rejected in the interest of other cargo loaded in the same space under deck. This applies especially to packages containing liquid cargoes.

The ship receives cargo, and receipts or bills of lading are signed for goods in 'apparent good order and condition'; if a bill of lading is so issued and the master accepts any package which does not correspond with this description he lays himself open to possible cargo claims which are not the fault of the ship but for which he must bear responsibility. The tally should therefore be claused in order that the condition of the goods may be inserted on the bill of lading.

Coal and grain cargoes are liable to spontaneous combustion as also is copra and cotton, and precautions must be taken to ensure the safe ventilation throughout the period of the voyage.

Grain, in addition to its natural tendency to become heated, is very liable to shift, and in charter-parties where full cargoes of bulk grain are carried the provision of shifting boards and/or alternatives such as strapping is included in the contract. Shifting boards are inserted in the holds dividing the space into several smaller compartments as an assistance to the stability of the ship if cargo should shift. Shifting boards or alternatives are now compulsory for most bulk grain cargoes.

A simple illustration of the ship if cargo should shift follows:

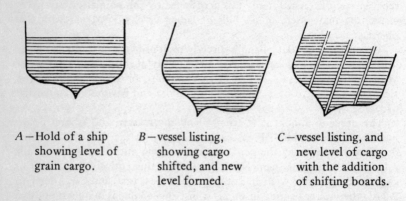

A — Hold of a ship showing level of grain cargo.

B — vessel listing, showing cargo shifted, and new level formed.

C — vessel listing, and new level of cargo with the addition of shifting boards.

From the second sketch (B) it will be seen that once a vessel has listed causing the cargo to find a new level it is a practical impossibility to right the ship to her original level, but in the last sketch where shifting boards are shown, it will be seen that although the vessel has listed and the cargo moved, the weight of the cargo is still evenly distributed, and the vessel will then regain her level immediately.

In grain cargoes also, the master usually has the right to demand a certain quantity of the cargo in bags, which he may stow in between and/ or on top of the bulk cargo thus forming divisions as an alternative, or assistance, to shifting boards, if these are not compulsorily required.

The latest regulations governing the shifting of bulk grain cargoes and its control as recommended by IMCO are contained in a Statutory Instrument of 1980, No. 536, entitled Merchant Shipping (Grain) Regulations 1980, which came into force 25 May 1980. For the above regulations 'grain' is defined as wheat, maize, oats, rye, barley, pulses and seeds.

In the regulations great stress is laid on trimming to level all free grain surfaces (loaded in bulk) to prevent it shifting.

In a ship whose construction includes an intermediate deck or decks, grain feeder hatches are provided to allow the nearly complete filling of any bulk cargo loaded by giving access to the wings etc. Bagged grain or strapping is also used to restrain the bulk cargo from shifting.

In any compartment of a ship which is only partly loaded, apart from trimming, the regulations lay down that the overstowing by other cargo and/or strapping and lashing to secure the cargo is compulsory.

These latest regulations require the carrying on board of a certificate (and the calculations which should accompany it) that the ship is capable of complying with the International Convention for the Safety of Life at Sea 1960, and on request the certification shall be produced by the Master to a Department of Trade Marine Surveyor. The issuing authorities of such certification are the Registration Societies. A 'Grain Certificate' is issued by the Canadian or US authorities, but the above certification that a designated ship can comply with the new regulations is now adequate in the UK and most other governmental signatories to the convention.

This tendency to shifting of cargo not only applies to grain but to many other types of cargo such as ores, flint stones, or small coal.

Holds may become tainted by the carrying of certain types of cargo, and be deemed unseaworthy for the reception of other cargo until all trace of the original cargo has been removed. It has already been mentioned that when cattle have been carried and foot and mouth disease has broken out, a ship is unseaworthy to load other cattle until such time as all trace of the infection has been removed and the vessel satisfactorily fumigated. Even some disinfectants themselves have strong odours and these must be dispersed before cargoes which might be affected are loaded in spaces or compartments so treated.

Any cargo which has a distinct odour should either be refused or carried only on deck, otherwise it will be found that other cargo stowed in the same space will become tainted by such odour. Any type of cargo containing creosote, as creosote in drums, or creosoted sleepers, has an effect on other cargo shipped in the same hold which when discharged will more often than not be found to have become tainted by the odour of the creosote. In addition to this there are many cargoes which are known for their natural tendency to affect other cargoes. Special provision should be made for the carriage of such dirty or objectionable cargo.

Provisions, butter, or any cargo which may be liable to melt or deteriorate if placed in contact with heat, should be stowed well away from boilers or parts of the ship which may be affected by heat from the ship's engines. The existence of a bulkhead dividing cargo from engines is not always sufficient to ensure freedom from damage due to this cause.

Reference has already been made in chapter 6 to the provisions of Para. 6 of Article 4 of the Carriage of Goods by Sea Act, with relation to dangerous cargoes. Other provisions are contained in Sects 446–450 of the Merchant Shipping Act 1894. The following is a summary of Sects 446–450 of the 1894 Act:

(1) It is unlawful to send or attempt to send or to carry or attempt to carry in any vessel any dangerous goods, without distinctly marking their nature on the outside of the package, and giving notice of their nature to the master or owner of the vessel at or before the time of sending them to be shipped. Breach of the above requirements renders the guilty person liable to a fine of £1000.

(2) To send or attempt to send dangerous goods under a false description renders the guilty person liable to a fine of £1000.

(3) The master or owner of a vessel is empowered to refuse any package which he suspects to contain dangerous goods and may require it to be opened to ascertain that fact. Where goods which the master or owner of the vessel deems to be dangerous have been sent or brought aboard a vessel without being marked or without notice being given, the master or owner may cause the goods to be thrown overboard, and shall not thereby be subject to either civil or criminal liability.

(4) Any court having Admiralty jurisdiction may declare goods wrongly taken on board under the above provisions to be forfeited and in such a case they may be disposed of as the court directs.

Seasonal shipments affect the general movement of cargoes, and it should be remembered that summer in countries south of the Equator extends from October to March, and with the cessation of harvest in the north, the south commences to become the provider of the world's needs.

This seasonal change and time of shipment of cargoes from certain places was more clearly defined some years ago than at present. Now, with the advent of cold stores, canning stations, refrigerator ships, and many other inventions and improvements, the markets of the world have become generalized, shipments being made at all times of the year.

A few seasons are given below:

GRAIN	CANADA. W. Coast Vancouver	March
	E. Coast Montreal	April F.O.W.
	PAKISTAN/ Karachi	March—May
	DANUBE	March
SUGAR	JAVA	November—December
	MAURITIUS	January
	CUBA	January—March
	WEST INDIES	January—March
WOOL	AUSTRALIA AND NEW ZEALAND	December—January
	(Two seasons)	October—November
	ARGENTINA AND SOUTH AFRICA	December and August
	KARACHI	March and August
COTTON	GULF OF MEXICO	May—October
TIMBER	BALTIC	April—May
		September—October
	GULF OF ST. LAWRENCE	April—May
		September—October
	GULF OF MEXICO	October—November
		March—April
	BURMA (Hardwoods)	August—September
	GULF OF NIGERIA (Mahogany) . .	January—February
	NORTHERN RANGE PORTS	October—November
		March—April

TEA	CHINA	February—March
	(New season crop. Indian slightly	October—November
	advanced to China)	
COCOA	WEST AFRICA	November—December
		March—April
	WEST INDIES	October—November
COFFEE	BRAZIL, AFRICA, INDIA, KENYA,	October—January
	AND CENTRAL AMERICAN	May—July
	STATES	

Cargo Information

The following particulars are given showing the places of shipment, how the cargo is packed, and the approximate stowage figures. These figures indicate the space occupied in a ship's hold by one ton of cargo (2240 lb) of the commodity mentioned. It will be seen that heavy cargoes occupy the smallest space, whilst the lighter the cargo is, the more space is occupied. From this will be seen the reason why when dealing with general cargoes or light cargoes that 'tween deck or shelter deck ships are required providing ample under deck space, against the single deck ships for heavy cargoes, where plenty of space is not necessary.

Apples—

From Canada, South Africa, Australia and New Zealand, Argentina, and the United States of America.
In boxes, 78 cu. ft. (2.208 cu. m.)
Increasing tendency, now almost common to ship only in cartons (on pallets). Cartons being of standard sizes to market requirements and contents being pre-graded. The cartons are marked by 'count', i.e. the number of individual fruit per carton. The weight per carton may vary, dependent upon the count. The cubic measurement of carton packed fruit is fairly comparable to that when in boxes.
In barrels, 90 cu. ft. (2.547 cu. m.)

Butter—

From Australia, Argentina, Denmark, New Zealand, United States of America, and Canada.
In cases, 60 cu. ft. (1.699 cu. m.)
In boxes, 55 cu. ft. (1.557 cu. m.)
In kegs, 65 cu. ft. (1.840 cu. m.)

Bananas—

West Indies, Surinam, West Africa, and Canaries.
In crates (single and double), 112 cu. ft. (3.171 cu. m.); or stems in plastic

bags. Bananas are now seldom shipped on stems hung in ships' holds, but are packed as bunches in cartons to predetermined weights. These vary slightly as to carton sizes and weights dependent upon differing arrangements in countries of origin.

Cotton—

Egypt, Sudan, America, India, Australia, Brazil, and Argentina.
Packed in bales.
Egypt, 70 cu. ft. (1.982 cu. m.). Each bale weighs 700 lb (317.52 kg).
Sudan, 90—100 cu. ft. (2.548—2.831 cu. m.)
America (New Orleans and Galveston), in bales of 480 lb. in two grades. Standard Egyptian, 150 cu. ft. (4.247 cu. m.), and high density, 85 cu. ft. (2.406 cu. m.)
India (Calcutta), Pakistan (Karachi), in bales, 55—60 cu. ft. (1.557—1.699 cu. m.)
Australia, 130 cu. ft. (3.681 cu. m.)

Copra—

Indonesia, Bangladesh, Malabar Coast, Malaysia, West Africa, and Oceania.
In sacks, 85—125 cu. ft. (2.406—3.539 cu. m.)
In cases, 80—90 cu. ft. (2.265—2.548 cu. m.)
In bulk, 70—120 cu. ft. (1.982—3.398 cu. m.)

Currants (dried)—

From Greece, 50 cu. ft. (1.415 cu. m.)
Australia and South Africa, 55 cu. ft. (1.557 cu. m.)
Packed in boxes.

Citrus Fruit—

From Africa, West Indies, United States of America, Atlantic islands, and Mediterranean ports, 68 cu. ft. (1.925 cu. m.)
Each case weighs 80 lb. (36.287 kg), and 17 standard cases measure 1 ton.
(See remarks under Apples. The same situation applies with carton packing of citrus fruits.)

Deals, Boards, and Battens—

Measured and carried by the standard of 165 cu. ft. (4.672 cu. m.) per standard.

Esparto Grass—

In bales. Unpressed, 120 cu. ft. (3.398 cu. m.). Semi-pressed, 90 cu. ft. (2.548 cu. m.)
From Southern Europe and North Africa.

Fruit Pulp—

In large tins in cartons 50—55 cu.ft. (1.415—1.557 cu.m.)

Grain—

Wheat from the temperate climates.
Maize from the sub-tropical climates.
Wheat shipped from Canada (St. Lawrence), Northern Range ports and New Orleans of the United States of America, Danube, and Karachi.
Shipped in bags or bulk.
Wheat in bags, 50 cu.ft. (1.415 cu.m.); in bulk, 45 cu.ft. (1.274 cu.m.)
Maize in bags, 55 cu.ft. (1.557 cu.m.); in bulk, 48—52 cu.ft. (1.359—1.472 cu.m.)
Barley in bags, 70—75 cu.ft. (1.982—2.123 cu.m.); in bulk, 60—65 cu.ft. (1.699—1.840 cu.m.)
Oats (clipped) in bags, 70 cu.ft. (1.982 cu.m.); in bulk, 60 cu.ft. (1.699 cu.m.)
Oats (unclipped) in bags, 80 cu.ft. (2.265 cu.m.); in bulk, 70 cu.ft. (1.982 cu.m.)

Ground Nuts (Kernels)—

West Africa, Madras Coast.
In bags, 65—68 cu.ft. (1.840—1.925 cu.m.)

Hides—

River Plate, South Africa, Australia, and China.

Places where large cattle ranches are in existence usually ship hides, with the exception of Canada, where, although ranches are abundant, few shipments of hides are made. Similarly, where wool is shipped it is usual to find large quantities of mutton and lamb being exported, but one exception to this generalization is South Africa, where, although quantities of wool are shipped, little meat is exported. Here the sheep are bred for the production of wool.

Measurements of hides are:
Wet, loose, 45—55 cu.ft. (1.274—1.557 cu.m.)
Dry, loose, 180—200 cu.ft. (5.097—5.663 cu.m.)
Salted in barrels, 55—60 cu.ft. (1.557—1.699 cu.m.)
African non-pressed, 86 cu.ft. (2.435 cu.m.)
Pressed, 22 cu.ft. (0.622 cu.m.) per bale.
Indian hides are carried on scale.

Hops—

From the Mediterranean, United Kingdom, and United States of America.
In bales or bags, 250—275 cu.ft. (7.079—7.789 cu.m.)
Plenty of ventilation is necessary for this cargo.

Iron Ore—

Spain, North and West Africa, Sweden, North and South America.
Loaded by grabs or baskets, 20—25 cu. ft. (0.566—0.707 cu. m.); in bulk
  14—20 cu. ft. (0.396—0.566 cu. m.)
This type of cargo is slow in loading or discharge except when being dealt
  with at ports which have special appliances for this cargo.

Lemons—

West Indies, Guyana, Italy, Spain, Israel and USA.
Boxes, 85 cu. ft. (2.406 cu. m.)
In bags or sacks, 80 cu. ft. (2.265 cu. m.)
(See remarks *re* carton packing under Apples and Citrus Fruit.)

Linseed—

Bombay and Calcutta, 57 cu. ft. (1.614 cu. m.)
River Plate, Australia, New Zealand, Karachi, 60—65 cu. ft. (1.699—
  1.840 cu. m.)

Mineral Ores include the following—

Antimony, cobalt, copper, lead, manganese, nickel, silver, chrome, tin, and
  zinc.
In bulk, 15—20 cu. ft. (0.424—0.566 cu. m.)
In bags, 18—22 cu. ft. (0.509—0.622 cu. m.)

Oil Cakes—

From all ports shipping cotton.
Oil cakes are made from the residue of crushed cotton-seed or linseed.
Shipped in bags, this commodity measures approximately 50—60 cu. ft.
  (1.415—1.699 cu. m.)
Egyptian oil cakes are heaviest.

Pit Props—

From White Sea ports, France, and Portugal.
Average, 50 cu. ft. (1.415 cu. m.)

Phosphates—

Gulf of Mexico, Morocco, Oceania, and Tunis.
In bags, 45—55 cu. ft. (1.274—1.557 cu. m.)
In bulk, 33—35 cu. ft. (0.934—0.991 cu. m.)

Rubber—

From Malaysia, Indonesia, and West Coast of Africa.

Packed in bags, bales, or cases.
Bales, 75 cu. ft. (2.123 cu. m.)
Cases, 65 cu. ft. (1.840 cu. m.)
Bags, 70 cu. ft. (1.982 cu. m.)

Rice—

From Burma, China, United States of America, Guyana, Surinam, French Guyana and Japan.
Burma, in bags, 50 cu. ft. (1.415 cu. m.). Cleaned rice, 40—45 cu. ft. (1.132—1.274 cu. m.)
China and Japan, in bags, 60 cu. ft. (1.699 cu. m.)

Sago—

Taiwan, Burma, and Vietnam.
In bags, 55 cu. ft. (1.557 cu. m.); in casks, 60 cu. ft. (1.699 cu. m.)

Seeds—

From India, China, and West Africa.
Indian seeds are carried on scale.
Hemp, 70 cu. ft. (1.982 cu. m.); rapeseed, 60 cu. ft. (1.699 cu. m.); mixed seeds, 75—80 cu. ft. (2.123—2.265 cu. m.)

Sugar—

From Java, Madagascar, Argentina, Caribbean, Mauritius, South Africa, East Indies, and Australia.
Java shipments in bags or baskets: bags, 48—50 cu. ft. (1.359—1.415 cu. m.); baskets, 60—63 cu. ft. (1.699—1.783 cu. m.)
Madagascar and South Africa: in bags, 40—45 cu. ft. (1.132—1.274 cu. m.)
East Indies: 36—42 cu. ft. (1.019—1.189 cu. m.)
Shipped in bulk, varies, 39—44 cu. ft. (1.104—1.245 cu. m.)

Timber—

Scandinavia and White Sea, St. Lawrence, Pacific, and Northern Range ports of the United States of America.
Carried on measurement of 165 cu. ft. (4.672 cu. m.) per standard.
Much sawn timber as boards is now shipped in prepacked bundles of several tons weight each.

Tinned Fruit—

From Canada, Australia, South Africa, New Zealand, and America, 50—54 cu. ft. (1.415—1.529 cu. m.)

Wool—

From Australia, New Zealand, South Africa, River Plate, and Mediterranean. In press packed bales, double bags.

Greasy wool, 180—190 cu. ft. (5.097—5.380 cu. m.); scoured, 280 cu. ft. (7.928 cu. m.); undumped, 240 cu. ft. (6.796 cu. m.); African pressed bales: greasy, 200 cu. ft. (5.663 cu. m.); scoured, 270—280 cu. ft. (7.645—7.928 cu. m.)

Australian raw wool (dumped and greasy) is double-pressed, and measures only 92 cu. ft. (2.605 cu. m.) per ton.

22 Hazardous Cargo and Pollution

There was a time when little or no thought was given to the question of pollution of the environment, and very little indeed was done against polluting the sea. The disposal of the unwanted or inconvenient by-products of industry or even the waste products of life itself — especially since the industrial revolution — has now called for an entirely new industry, namely that of re-cycling. Many of these waste or surplus materials in the industrialized countries are now being converted into usable or totally inert products although certain characteristics of some items seem to defy the rendering of them harmless. However, the subject has now reached the point where consideration of most aspects of pollution control have been covered by legislation, particularly those associated with oil at sea.

Accidents to oil tankers, especially as these grew larger, caused widespread damage to fishing grounds and sea bird life, as well as the despoilation of beaches. Heavy penalties are now exacted from those responsible either by careless washing out of their tanks or by the results of faulty navigation. Accidents to oil or gas tankers are not the only source of sea pollution as ships carrying other cargoes such as drums of corrosive chemicals or poisons can also cause pollution.

Perhaps it will assist the student if a reminder of two or three causes of pollution are given.

In the case of the *Torrey Canyon* in March 1967, the ship was wrecked on the Seven Stones, off the Scilly Isles. It was a modern and well-found ship; the accident was the result of bad navigation. The ship's tanks were torn open, spilling upwards of 80,000 tons of oil, some of which came ashore amongst other places on the Cornish, Devon and Dorset coast and as far East as some parts of Hampshire, and also on the Brittany coast and Guernsey, with disasterous results to sea bird life and with widespread disfiguring of the coast. (An accident of this type had been contemplated for some time, but no-one knew for certain the extent of the despoilation which would arise.)

At the time various chemicals were used to disperse the oil at sea, at very considerable cost in terms of money and manpower, but the chemicals themselves created conditions where, for a limited period of time, the sea coast was denuded of small marine life. This in time passed away, but nowadays less initially harmful chemicals are used, and more attempts still are made to deal with the oil before it comes ashore.

Around the coasts of the UK at several selected ports, considerable stocks of dispersant chemicals are held and smaller ships such as tugs and fishing boats are fitted with the necessary spraying gear and when called upon they collect the stored chemicals and proceed to the scene of disaster and spray the surface of the sea to dissolve and disperse the oil. Obviously this action may not be wholly successful but it ameliorates substantially the situation which results from this form of accident.

A further example of potential sea pollution was identified when the Yugoslav *Cavtat* was sunk in July 1974 as the result of a collision near Cape Otranto in the Southern Adriatic. Part of the cargo consisted of some 900 drums of tetra-ethyl-lead and after a period it was decided to attempt to salvage these drums. As is known, tetra-ethyl-lead is very poisonous and the whole operation involved considerable risk to the salvage crew and very great cost but if it had not been undertaken, the fishing in that part of the sea would have been destroyed for years to come. In this case the corrosion of the wreck by being under the sea was of itself a risk, but it was accepted.

A further example is that of untreated sewage or only partially treated sewage, which heavily pollutes the sea water when dumped into the sea. This has been until recently a very considerable menace particularly in certain parts of the Mediterranean Sea. However a conference of states bordering that sea has been held and arrangements made to deal with the problem and also the raw and untreated industrial effluent which have together contributed to the situation. Because this problem is so large and yet so fragmented it will take years to rectify, as old-fashioned plant is trying to cope with it. But it has been recognized and steps taken to deal with it — steps differing in detail in each location of trouble, but coordinated in their effect.

Perhaps the best way of protecting the environment against thoughtless or neglectful pollution is by prevention rather than 'cure', but this does not remove the necessity of taking all possible precautions to limit the extent of disasters when they do overtake us.

The standard reference is the Carriage of Dangerous Goods in Ships (The Blue Book) of 1966; Statutory Instrument No. 1067 of 1965, entitled Merchant Shipping (Dangerous Goods) Rules 1965, operative on 26 May 1965, and subsequent Supplements.

At present many explosives, poisons, and hazardous or corrosive chemicals have special regulations governing their handling and transport by sea, even in small quantities, but many such as nuclear waste, remain outside of the scope of these regulations.

Students are unlikely to be closely concerned with these matters, but are advised that reference to the above book (and its Supplements) is helpful as to handling precautions, protective clothing, quantity limits etc., and they should then consult the Port Regulations of the intended destination to verify whether the commodities concerned have a limit of quantity differing from that of the proposed loading port or can only be received at some particular berth or are even entirely prohibited.

Dumping at sea is now in rather a special category. Permission has almost certainly to be obtained from governments; indeed it must be established whether dumping is permitted at all, and if so with what precautions; and where and when particular waste products can be dumped (e.g. in deep water). Certain types of nuclear waste fall into this category.

23 Agents and Agency

An agent is a person who acts for or on behalf of another (the principal) in such a manner that the principal is legally liable for all acts carried out under such agency.

There are several ways in which an agency may be created, and the rules apply not only to shipping but to all other commercial or professional agents.

The clearest manner in which an agency may be created is by *express* agreement, whereby the agent receives from his principal definite instructions to do certain things on his behalf. He will receive either limited bounds in which to operate or a general agency by which he may act in all manners in the furtherance of his principal's business.

Implied agency is created when a person receives implied authority to act for another; an example may be given in the case of the master of a vessel, who is the agent of the owners by appointment in relation to the conduct of the ship and ship's business. He is, however, only bailee for the cargo which is carried on board the ship. Under his powers as bailee, he has not authority to do other than care for and keep the goods in his charge until delivery. But when the ship meets with danger or in a time of peril, the master has implied authority to act as agent for the cargo owner, and may dispose of, or treat with the cargo, which in his ordinary course of business he would have no authority to do. It may be noted that the master has limited powers only in ordinary times, but in times of peril his authority is unlimited.

Agency by ratification occurs when the agent commits an act for which he has no authority whatsoever, but acquaints his principal *after the occurrence* with his act, and the principal agrees to and accepts the agent's action. A contract in excess of authority can be ratified only when the original agent contracted as agent, though in excess of authority.

The golden rule of agency may be expressed as: 'Never exceed instructions, and always keep within authority.' For an agent who acts upon these lines, there should never be any question of liability, or possible fear of the responsibility falling upon his shoulders.

When a principal appoints an agent, then all the acts of the agent, and responsibilities incurred are for account of the principal as though he had acted personally, but only when he has given his agent the power to act in such manner. Should the agent exceed his authority and carry out an action which is outside the scope of his agency then the principal may refuse to accept responsibility. It should be observed, however, that the principal cannot impose secret limitations on the power of the agent; any limitations must be communicated to the other party.

While the agent must act upon his instructions, he has implied powers given him to do everything necessary for the execution of any expressed authority he may have received. If the agent is appointed for the purpose of carrying out a certain duty, and receives authority to do so, but before he is able to proceed has to carry out other acts then his authority is implied for such acts, it being understood that he could not have proceeded with his agency until such matters were attended to.

A special point here which may be stressed is that whilst an agent receives authority to fix a charter-party, he has no authority to alter the charter-party in any manner after it has been signed, even if he sees that such an alteration is in his principal's interest. Having carried out his duty his responsibility ceases immediately.

There is also no authority given to an agent to delegate his duty to another person to act for him. Having been selected as the agent of the principal, then he must carry out such agency himself, and he has no powers of delegation unless express or implied authority to delegate has been given to him by the principal, or unless it is permissible by custom of trade, or unless the nature of the business requires delegation.

The mere fact of delegation does not as a rule establish any relationship between the principal and the sub-agent. The sub-agent is responsible only to the agent who appointed him, and the principal is not liable for the acts of the sub-agent. This is so even where the agent has authority to delegate. Where, however, the principal has definitely accepted and agreed to the sub-agent who is appointed a relationship may spring up directly between the principal and the sub-agent (there is said to be privity of contract between them), and in such case the original agent drops out and the sub-agent becomes in effect an agent.

The agent is not allowed to use any information which he may obtain from one principal in carrying out his duties with another principal. That is, any confidential information that is acquired whilst operating an agency for one person may not be used in connection with any agency with another. The use of experience and general information is not debarred, but only such information as, if used, might be detrimental to the principal from whom it was acquired.

Under the Prevention of Corruption Act 1906 an agent may not receive any secret commission, or payment from persons other than his principal. This is to prevent bribery and corruption as a means of securing or influencing business, and furthermore, should any agent be discovered to have accepted any such payments, then he must hand the sums received to his principal.

In effect, the agent is unable in the course of his duties to earn more than the amount which is allowed to him under his commission agreement.

Any increase in profits brings to him increase in commission, by which method he is repaid if the agency flourishes under his guidance. Where, for example, an agent receives goods for export at the agreed selling price of 50p, and he is able to dispose of the articles at 55p, then the addition resulting from the increased selling price must be credited to his principal, irrespective of the fact that the principal would be satisfied if he received only the 50p desired.

The agent has a right to his commission, which may be either at an expressed rate or implied; should there be no express agreement, then the right to commission is implied at such a rate as is customary or usual.

It is usual to incorporate in the charter-party a clause providing for the agent's commission—in such a case the agent cannot himself sue on the charter-party as he is not a party to it; he may, however, sue through his principal as trustee for him, and in any event he can sue his principal on a collateral agreement to pay his commission evidenced in the charter-party. If the charter-party contains no reference to the agent's commission he may sue the shipowner on an implied contract to pay him the customary remuneration.

Whilst the principal is responsible to the agent for payment of all commission due, there is no obligation on the part of the principal to continue a contract for the sole benefit of an agent earning his commission. For example, where a long time charter-party has been fixed for ten years the agent may consider that for this period he will receive commission. Should the principals agree mutually to close the contract after two years have elapsed, they may do so, and the agent is therefore placed in the position of losing eight years' commission. The agent in such a case has no remedy unless a clause is inserted in the charter-party or agency agreement whereby he is to receive commission for the full time of the contract. A point here to be emphasized, however, is that there must be no collaboration on the part of the principals to close the contract in order that the agent's right to his commission shall be defeated.

The agents concerned with the chartering of vessels are known as brokers, and many charter-parties are fixed by the brokers acting on behalf of the principals. In this case the broker should see that his signature to a charter-party is clearly defined, stating that he is an agent, and he must therefore sign the document and qualify his signature by the words 'as agents', 'as agents for the charterers', or by any similar words. The use of the word 'agent' alone is considered as only a description and not as a qualifying word. This procedure need not be adopted when there is reference made in the body of the document to the fact that the person executing it is an agent. If, for example, 'A.B.' is referred to in the body of charter-party as agent for 'C.D.' then there is no necessity for 'A.B.' to qualify his signature when completing the document, as it has been held that the document is construed as a whole in all cases of dispute.

As in the case of many other contracts by brokers, charter-parties are arranged by telephone or telegraphic communication, and the broker must in these cases (to ensure his own safety), qualify his signature by such words as 'by telegraphic authority', or 'by telephonic authority', or again in some cases 'Subject to owner's approval'. In each case the agent makes allowance for any discrepancies which may have occured in the course of transmission of the cables or telegram.

When an agent works under the conditions which have been emphasized above, he may have little or no fear that any acts of his own will render him personally liable.

24 Protection and Indemnity Clubs

These clubs, which are known by the short title of 'P. & I. Clubs', are formed by the shipowners in order to secure cover for risks which are outside the normal marine insurance policy, risks which perhaps may be more clearly understood as third party risks.

'War Risk Clubs' are clubs organized for a like purpose in war time and are run in a similar way, and although not operating in peace time, are still kept in existence.

The maintenance of these clubs is secured by way of a levy upon the amount of tonnage owned by the members of the club, each making his proportionate payment to the funds to the club.

Shipowners having realized that they have not been able to secure cover by insurance for certain risks, become members of these clubs and by so doing obtain the necessary security against possible loss, thus avoiding any financial setback which they are liable to receive if they do not take advantage of this method.

It must not be assumed that because a shipowner is a member of one of these clubs he may automatically dip in his hands and collect his losses; the money which he draws out must be replaced sooner or later, consequently, the more the members receive out of these clubs, the more they must pay into them, to ensure the organization remaining solvent.

Calls are made from time to time by the secretaries of the clubs; by this method they replenish their funds and, consequently, when several severe losses follow one another the calls made by the clubs become correspondingly heavy.

The clubs are divided into two sections, namely, Protection and Indemnity, and usually cover the following risks:

Protection

Cases of loss of life or personal injury.

Repatriation of distressed seamen, and any expenses for hospital and medical attention.

Loss of life following collision.

Loss or damage by collision to another vessel, including one-quarter of

126

the value of the cargo on board — it being remembered that three-quarters of the cargo is covered under the marine policies.
Loss or damage to cargo arising from improper navigation.
Cargo's proportion of general average arising from improper navigation.
Damage to piers, jetties, and wharves.
Cost of raising wreck.
Cost of Department of Trade inquiries.
Quarantine expenses.
Legal costs of defending claims.

Indemnity

Wrong, short, or mixed delivery of cargo.
Ship's liability following collision, which is not covered by insurance.
Cost of fines which may be caused by the barratry and wrongful acts of the master and/or crew.
Cost of resisting cargo claims.

The cost of defending and resisting claims which is mentioned at the close of each section does not refer to the ordinary commercial claims which an owner has to contend with, but only to claims which have significance in the interest of all owners.

Such cases, when fought, may usually be described as 'test' cases in which owners are desirous of obtaining a legal ruling upon a certain matter by which they may be guided in the future. These test cases may cost some thousands of pounds before they are settled, and may appear an extravagant expense of money, but when it is realized that stated rulings are laid down on which owners may act in future similar circumstances thus obviating many claims of a like nature, this expense appears obviously necessary.

25 Arbitration

The usefulness and significance of arbitration is demonstrated by its increasing use by the business community and the legal profession in many countries of the world. The primary advantage is the speed with which controversies can be resolved by arbitration, compared with the long delays of ordinary court procedure. The expert technical knowledge of arbitrators and their knowledge of the customs and usages of the specific trade makes testimony by others and much documentation unnecessary, thereby eliminating expenses connected with court procedures. The privacy of the arbitration procedure is also much valued by the parties to a controversy.

Arbitration is a legal technique for resolving disputes by referring them to a third party for a binding decision, or 'award', as an arbitrator's findings are described. The 'arbitrator' may be a single person or an arbitration tribunal usually of three members. Arbitration must be distinguished from conciliation and mediation whereby parties resort to a third person to help them to reach a compromise or to offer a recommendation for a settlement. Such intervention by a third party has no binding force upon the disputants, as has the arbitrator's decision, the 'award'.

Arbitration is most commonly resorted to for the resolution of commercial disputes. Conciliation and mediation are more common in the settlement of labour disputes between management and labour unions although the process is often referred to erroneously as 'arbitration'. Increasingly, however, conciliation and mediation are being used in commercial disputes as a first attempt at dispute resolution, as any rights of the parties to resort to arbitration or litigation should a settlement not be achieved, are in no way affected.

The settlement of disputes, whether commercial or otherwise, by arbitration has been common in England for centuries. Between the first Arbitration Act of 1698 and the codification of the law of arbitration by the Arbitration Act of 1950, there were four other acts of Parliament relating to arbitration under the laws of England. These were the Civil Procedure Act 1833; the Common Law Procedure Act 1854; the Judicate Acts of 1873 and 1884; the Arbitration Act 1889 and the Arbitration Act 1934. The 1950 Arbitration Act is now the Principal Act and there are two further acts which supplement or amend this act, these are the 1975 and 1979 Acts.

The 1950 Arbitration Act provides that, unless a contrary interim is expressed in the agreement, the authority of an arbitrator or umpire appointed by, or by virtue of, an arbitration agreement shall be irrevocable except by leave of the High Court or a judge thereof. The High Court may remove an arbitrator or umpire who has misconducted himself, or the proceedings and may set aside an award in such a case.

The Arbitration Act 1950 gives the arbitrator or umpire important powers in regard to, inter alia, the production of documents by the parties and the giving of evidence in the arbitration. It also provides that an arbitration agreement or an award may, by leave of the High Court, be enforced in the same manner as a judgment or order to the same effect.

The 1958 United Nations Convention for the Recognition and Enforcement of Arbitral Award (known as the 1958 New York Convention) facilitates the enforcement of international arbitral awards as the Convention has been ratified by the governments of over 80 countries. The 1979 Arbitration Act enables overseas parties to a dispute to opt out of judicial review by the English Courts. It also provides for a new procedure of judicial review for 'domestic' (i.e., where no overseas party is involved) disputes and for international arbitrations where there is no 'exclusion agreement'.

There is an increasing tendency for arbitration to be conducted under a set of rules which supplement the 1950 Arbitration Act, such as those of the London Court of Arbitration and the Chartered Institute of Arbitrators. These rules provide for general arbitrations, international arbitrations and small claims arbitrations. They also incorporate the United Nations Arbitration Rules (the UNCITRAL Rules). Where parties to a dispute opt for the arbitration to be conducted under a set of rules such as those mentioned above, there are considerable advantages as the parties are aware in advance of the procedures to be adopted and timetables are set to ensure steady and uninterrupted progress toward a final and binding award.

26 Definitions and Abbreviations

a.a. Always afloat. Provision in charter-party that the vessel must remain afloat at all times when loading and discharging.

A. & C.P. Anchors and chains proved.

Abandonment. To give up the possession of a vessel, usually when in a position of danger.

Act of God. Any act which could not have been prevented by human intervention or forethought.

Ad valorem. According to the value.

Ad valorem duty. A duty based upon the value of the goods.

Ad valorem freight. Freight chargeable on the value of the goods shipped and not on weight or measurement.

Advance notes. A draft upon the owners of a vessel for wages in advance given to the seaman upon signing articles.

a.f. Advance freight. Freight paid in advance.

Affreightment. A contract for the carriage of goods by sea, expressed in a charter-party, or by the terms and conditions of a bill of lading.

A/H. Antwerp-Hamburg range.

A.M. American Bureau of Shipping.

Arbitration. The process of submitting matters of dispute or of a controversial nature to the judgment of an agreed person, or persons, without applying to courts for a settlement.

Arbitration award. The decision of arbitrator(s).

Bailee. Person to whom goods are entrusted for a special purpose.

Barratry. Fraudulent act on the part of the master and/or crew of a vessel without the connivance of the owners.

B.C. Bristol Channel.

B.D. Bar draft. The amount of water over a bar measured at the ebb tide.

B.E. Bill of entry; or bill of exchange.

B.H. Bill of health. Certificate issued by the Medical Officer of Health for the port, giving a statement of the condition of the health of the port or ship.

B/L. Bill of lading. A receipt for goods received for shipment or shipped on board a vessel. It is a document of title, and whilst not a contract, contains *prima facie* evidence of the terms and conditions of such.

Bonded goods. Goods deposited in a bonded warehouse until such time as the duty upon them has been paid.

B.o.T. Board of Trade. (Now **D.o.T.**, Department of Trade.)

Bottomry. Money borrowed upon a ship's hull, gear, and cargo which is repayable with interest when the vessel returns to port in safety. It is forfeited should the vessel sink.

Brokerage. Commission charged for securing and transacting business connected with shipping.

B/S. Bill of sale.

b.t. Berth terms.

Bunker. Space in which the fuel for the vessel is stored, or the actual fuel itself.

B.V. Bureau Veritas.

Cargo. Merchandise for carriage on board a ship.

C. & F. Cost and freight.

C. & I. Cost and insurance.

Caveat Emptor. Let the buyer beware. The purchaser must ascertain the state and condition of the goods before he makes the purchase.

C.C. Civil commotion.

Cesser clause. This clause relieves the charterer from liability after loading of cargo, and payment of freight, dead freight, and demurrage.

C.F.O. Calling for orders.

Charter-party. A contract between shipowner and charterer for the carriage of goods, or hire of vessel, for a period of time.

C.I.F. Cost, insurance, and freight.

C.I.F.C.I. Cost, insurance, freight, commission, and interest.

C.I.F.L.T. Cost, insurance, freight, London terms.

Clearance. Official permission from customs officer for a vessel to leave port when all dues have been paid, and all formalities observed.

Clear days. Time to be reckoned exclusive of the first and last days.

Complement. The number of crew employed upon a vessel for its safe navigation.

Consign. To send goods from one place to another.

Consignor. The person who consigns or forwards the goods.

Consignee. The person to whom the goods are sent.

Consul. The commercial representative of one nation residing officially in another country, to facilitate business relations between the two countries.

Consulage. Fees paid to a consul for protection of goods, or signing of documents or other services.

Cont. B/H. Continent, Bordeaux-Hamburg range.

Cont. H/H. Continent, Havre-Hamburg range.

Contraband. Goods smuggled into a country avoiding duty.

c.p.d. Charterers pay dues.

C.T.L. Constructive total loss.

c.t.l.o. Constructive total loss only.

cu. ft. Cubic feet, 40 cu. ft. being the basis of a freight ton.

D.B.B. Deals, boards, and battens.

D.C. Deviation clause.

dd. Delivered.

Deadfreight. Freight paid for space booked but not used.

Deck load. Cargo carried upon deck.

Del credere. An agreement by which an agent when he sells goods on credit for an additional commission, guarantees solvency of the buyer, and his performance of the contract.

Demurrage. Compensation paid to shipowner for delay of a vessel beyond the stipulated time in charter-party for loading or discharge.

Deviation. Departure from the set or agreed course of the voyage.

Dirty money. Extra payment to labourers for handling goods of an objectionable nature.

Dispatch money. Bonus paid to charterer for loading and/or discharging a vessel in less time than stipulated in charter-party.

dp. Direct port.

D.O.T. or **D. of T.** Department of Trade.

Drawback. Allowance granted by Government to encourage the exportation of certain articles, or a return of duty paid on certain articles.

Dreadage. The option of shipping general cargo under a grain charter-party. Freight to be paid at the same rate as grain, but all extra charges incurred to be for account of the charterers.

Dock dues. Charges made upon shipping for the use of docks.

Draught. Depth of water necessary to float a vessel.

Dumb barge. Barge without sail or motive power.

Dunnage. Material (wood, matting, etc.) used in stowing cargo either for separation or for prevention of damage.

d.w.c.c. Dead weight cargo capacity.

E.C.C.P. East Coast coal port.

E.C.U.K. East Coast, United Kingdom.

Embargo. Government order for prohibition against sailing of vessels from or to a certain port.

ex. Out of.

Excise. Duty charged on home produced goods before sale to consumer.

Ex facie. According to documents.

Ex quay. Buyer is responsible for charges after delivery on quay.

Ex ship. Seller pays freight to port of destination. All other charges for account of the purchaser.

F. & d. Freight and demurrage.

f.a. Free alongside.

f.a.c. Fast as can.

f.c. & s. Free of capture and seizure.

f.d. Free delivery; or free dispatch.

f.i.b. Free into bunkers; or free into barge.

f.i.o. Free in and out.

Flotsam. Goods lost by shipwreck and found floating on sea.

f.o.b. Free on board.

f.o.c. Free of charge.

Founder. To fill with water and sink.

f.o.w. First open water. A term used in connection with ice-bound ports.

f.o.d. Free of damage.

Form O. American charter-party for cotton trade.

Franco. Prepaid.

f.r. & c.c. Free of riots and civil commotion.

frt. Freight.

f.t. Free turn; or full terms.

G/A. General average.

G.C.B.S. General Council of British Shipping.

Gross tonnage. Vessel's internal space measured in units of 100 cu. ft.

Groundage. Charge made for permission to anchor.

Hogged. When the two ends of the ship droop lower than the part amidships.

Hold. A part of the interior of a vessel below decks in which cargo may be stowed.

Home trade. British Isles and Elbe-Brest range of ports inclusive.

I.M.C.O. Inter-governmental Maritime Consultative Organization.

Indemnity. Security of compensation against loss or damage.

Inherent vice. Defect due to the nature of the object or goods.

In transitu. On the passage.

Inward charges. Charges incurred on a ship entering a port, e.g. pilotage, etc.

i.v. Invoice value.

Jetsam. Goods which have been thrown overboard for the purpose of lightening the ship.

Jettison. To throw overboard.

j. & w.o. Jettison and washing overboard.

Knot. A marine measure of speed, being one nautical mile of 6080 ft. traversed in one hour.

Lagan. Goods jettisoned, but which have a floating object attached by which they may be recovered.

Landing order. Authority to dock company or wharfinger to receive goods from a ship.

Lay days. Days allowed for loading or discharging of a vessel under charter-party.

Lazaretto. Part of the ship in which persons under quarantine regulations are quartered, or the place where goods are fumigated.

L.C. London clause.

L.E.F.O. Lands End for Orders.

Levant. Eastern end of the Mediterranean, including islands.

Lien. The right of holding goods until a debt due in respect to such goods is satisfied.

Light dues. Tolls levied on vessels for the purchase of maintaining light-houses and lightships.

Lighterage. Charge for the use of a barge or lighter.

L.M.C. Lloyd's machinery certificate.

L.L.T. London landed terms.

Loading turn. Rotation or order for ships to berth and load cargo.

London clause. 'The shipowner shall be entitled to land these goods on the quays or the dock when ship discharges immediately on arrival, and upon the goods being so landed the shipowner's responsibility ceases. This clause is to form part of the bill of lading and any words at variance with it are hereby cancelled.'

L.R. Lloyd's Register (of Shipping).

L.R.M.C. Lloyd's Refrigerating Machinery Certificate.

Lump sum freight. Gross sum of money stipulated to be paid for the carriage of cargo, irrespective of quantity.

Metric ton. 2204.6223 lb.

M/R. Mate's receipt.

n.a.a. Not always afloat.

n.d. Non-delivery.

N.M.B. National Maritime Board.

n/n. Not north of.

n.o.p. Not otherwise provided.

Not negotiable. Cannot be transferred to any other person with the same rights as were held by the original owner.

n.r. Net register.

n.r.a.d. No risk after discharge.

n.r.a.l. No risk after landing.

n.r.a.s. No risk after shipment.

Northern range. The US ports of Norfolk, Newport News, Baltimore, Philadelphia, New York, Boston, and Portland (Maine).

n.t. Net terms.

Open charter. Charter-party whereby vessel may fix for any cargo and for any ports.

p/a. Particular average.

P. & I. Protection and indemnity.

p.o.c. Port of call.

Poop. Raised deck at stern of vessel.

p.o.r. Port of refuge.

Portage bill. The account of members of the crew of a vessel, giving particulars of wages, allowances, etc.

Pratique. The permit for a vessel to communicate with land after a clean bill of health has been produced, or quarantine restrictions have been observed.

Prima facie. At the first glance; on the face of it.

Primage. Percentage added to the freight and retained by the loading broker; recoverable in part or in all as rebate according to the regulations of the conference under which vessel is operating.

Pro forma. As a matter of form.

Pro rata. In the proportion to.

Quoin. A wooden wedge used for chocking barrels to prevent movement.

r.d. Running days.

r.d.c. Running down clause.

Rebate. Allowance or discount made.

r.o.b. Remaining on board.

Sabotage. Wilful destruction.

Safe port. Port where a vessel may lie without danger from physical or political interference.

s.b.s. Surveyed before shipment.

Scuttle. To let water into a ship for the purpose of sinking.

s.d. Short delivery.

S/H.E. or SHEX. Sundays and holidays excepted.

SHINC. Sundays and holidays included.

Shipping note. A receipt note giving particulars of goods forwarded to a dock for shipment.

SITPRO. Simplification of International Trade Procedure Board.

SOLAS Safety of Life at Sea (Regulations).

s.p.d. Ship pays dues.

Spot. Ready to load.

std. Standard. (165 cu. ft. – timber measurement)

Stevedore. Person who acts as a contractor for or supervisor of labour in loading or discharging vessels in port.

Stripping. Devanning or emptying containers.

Stuffing. Loading containers.

Supercargo. Person engaged on a vessel for the purpose of superintending the cargo, its disposal and care to the best advantage.

Tallying. The act of checking goods loaded on or discharged from a vessel.

T. & p. Theft and pilferage.

T. & S. Touch and stay.

Tare. Weight of a container when empty.

Tariff. List of duties payable on goods. List of freight rates issued and agreed by a shipping conference.

T.l. Total loss.

T.l.o. Total loss only.

T/O. Transfer Order.

t.p.i. Tons per inch (immersion).

Transhipment. The removal of goods from one vessel to another, or carriage from port of discharge to a further destination.

Tret. Allowance for ordinary wear and tear or depreciation during a voyage.

T.T. Telegraphic transfer (of money).

T.W.H.D. Tons per workable hatch per day.

U.K.F.O. United Kingdom for orders.

Ullage. Quantity a cask or drum lacks of being full.

U.S.N.H. United States North of (Cape) Hatteras.

Vice propre. Inherent vice.
W.b. Water ballast.
W.C.E. West Coast of England.
W/M. Weight and/or measurement.
W.N.A. Winter, North Atlantic.
W.p. Without prejudice.
w.w.d. Weather working day.
Y.A.R. York-Antwerp Rules.

Appendix A Carriage of Goods by Sea Act 1971

An Act to amend the law with respect to the carriage of goods by sea.

1.—(1) In this Act, 'the Rules' means the International Convention for the unification of certain rules of law relating to bills of lading signed at Brussels on 25 August 1924, as amended by the Protocol signed at Brussels on 23 February 1968.

(2) The provisions of the Rules, as set out in the Schedule in this Act, shall have the force of law.

(3) Without prejudice to subsection (2) above, the said provisions shall have effect (and have the force of law) in relation to and in connection with the carriage of goods by sea in ships where the port of shipment is a port in the United Kingdom, whether or not the carriage is between ports in two different States within the meaning of Article X of the Rules.

(4) Subject to subsection (6) below, nothing in this section shall be taken as applying anything in the Rules to any contract for the carriage of goods by sea, unless the contract expressly or by implication provides for the issue of a bill of lading or any similar document of title.

(5) The Secretary of State may from time to time by order made by statutory instrument specify the respective amounts which for the purposes of paragraph 5 of Article IV of the Rules and of Article IV bis of the Rules are to be taken as equivalent to the sums expressed in francs which are mentioned in sub-paragraph (*a*) of that paragraph.

(6) Without prejudice to Article X(*c*) of the Rules, the Rules shall have the force of law in relation to:

(*a*) any bill of lading if the contract contained in or evidenced by it expressly provides that the Rules shall govern the contract, and

(*b*) any receipt which is a non-negotiable document marked as such if the contract contained in or evidenced by it is a contract for the carriage of goods by sea which expressly provides that the Rules are to govern the contract as if the receipt were a bill of lading,

but subject, where paragraph (*b*) applies, to any necessary modifications and in particular with the omission in Article III of the Rules of the second sentence of paragraph 4 and of paragraph 7.

(7) If and so far as the contract contained in or evidenced by a bill of lading or receipt within paragraph (*a*) or (*b*) of subsection (6) above applies to deck cargo or live animals, the Rules as given the force of law by

that subsection shall have effect as if Article I(*c*) did not exclude deck cargo and live animals.

In this subsection 'deck cargo' means cargo which by the contract of carriage is stated as being carried on deck and is so carried.

2.—(1) If Her Majesty by Order in Council certifies to the following effect, that is to say, that for the purposes of the Rules:

(*a*) a State specified in the Order is a contracting State, or is a contracting State in respect of any place or territory so specified; or

(*b*) any place or territory specified in the Order forms part of a State so specified (whether a contracting State or not)

the Order shall, except so far as it has been superseded by a subsequent Order, be conclusive evidence of the matters so certified.

(2) An Order in Council under this section may be varied or revoked by a subsequent Order in Council.

3. There shall not be implied in any contract for the carriage of goods by sea to which the Rules apply by virtue of this Act any absolute undertaking by the carrier of the goods to provide a seaworthy ship.

4.—(1) Her Majesty may by Order in Council direct that this Act shall extend, subject to such exceptions, adaptations and modifications as may be specified in the Order, to all or any of the following territories, that is:

(*a*) any colony (not being a colony for whose external relations a country other than the United Kingdom is responsible),

(*b*) any country outside Her Majesty's dominions in which Her Majesty has jurisdiction in right of Her Majesty's Government of the United Kingdom.

(2) An order in Council under this section may contain such transitional and other consequental and incidental provisions as appear to Her Majesty to be expedient, including provisions amending or repealing any legislation about the carriage of goods by sea forming part of the law of any of the territories mentioned in paragraphs (*a*) and (*b*) above.

(3) An Order in Council under this section may be varied or revoked by a subsequent Order in Council.

5.—(1) Her Majesty may by Order in Council provide that section 1(3) of this Act shall have effect as if the reference therein to the United Kingdom included a reference to all or any of the following territories, that is:

(*a*) the Isle of Man;

(*b*) any of the Channel Islands specified in the Order;

(*c*) any colony specified in the Order (not being a colony for whose external relations a country other than the United Kingdom is responsible);

(*d*) any associated state (as defined by section 1(3) of the West Indies Act 1967) specified in the Order;

(*e*) any country specified in the Order, being a country outside Her Majesty's dominions in which Her Majesty has jurisdiction in right of Her Majesty's Government of the United Kingdom.

(2) An Order in Council under this section may be varied or revoked by a subsequent Order in Council.

6.—(1) This Act may be cited as the Carriage of Goods by Sea Act 1971.

(2) It is hereby declared that this Act extends to Northern Ireland.

(3) The following enactments shall be repealed, that is:

    (*a*) the Carriage of Goods by Sea Act 1924,

    (*b*) section 12(4)(*a*) of the Nuclear Installations Act 1965,

and without prejudice to section 38(1) of the Interpretation Act 1889, the reference to the said Act of 1924 in section 1(1)(*i*)(ii) of the Hovercraft Act 1968 shall include a reference to this Act.

(4) It is hereby declared that for the purposes of Article VIII of the Rules section 502 of the Merchant Shipping Act 1894 (which, as amended by the Merchant Shipping (Liability of Shipowners and Others) Act 1958, entirely exempts shipowners and others in certain circumstances from liability for loss of, or damage to, goods) is a provision relating to limitation of liability.

(5) This Act shall come into force on such day as Her Majesty may by Order in Council appoint, and, for the purpose of the transition from the law in force immediately before the day appointed under this subsection to the provisions of this Act, the Order appointing the day may provide that those provisions shall have effect subject to such transitional provisions as may be contained in the Order.

Schedule: the Hague Rules as amended by the Brussels Protocol 1968

Article I

In these Rules the following words are employed, with the meanings set out below:

    (*a*) 'Carrier' includes the owner or the charterer who enters into a contract of carriage with a shipper.

    (*b*) 'Contract of carriage' applies only to contracts of carriage covered by a bill of lading or any similar document of title, in so far as such document relates to the carriage of goods by sea, including any bill of lading or any similar document as aforesaid issued under or pursuant to a charter-party from the moment at which such bill of lading or similar document of title regulates the relations between a carrier and a holder of the same.

    (*c*) 'Goods' includes goods, wares, merchandise, and articles of every kind whatsoever except live animals and cargo which by the contract of carriage is stated as being carried on deck and is so carried.

    (*d*) 'Ship' means any vessel used for the carriage of goods by sea.

    (*e*) 'Carriage of goods' covers the period from the time when the goods are loaded on to the time they are discharged from the ship.

Article II

Subject to the provisions of Article VI, under every contract of carriage of goods by sea the carrier, in relation to the loading, handling, stowage, carriage, custody, care and discharge of such goods, shall be subject to the responsibilities and liabilities, and entitled to the rights and immunities hereinafter set forth.

Article III

1. The carrier shall be bound before and at the beginning of the voyage to exercise due diligence to:

(*a*) Make the ship seaworthy.

(*b*) Properly man, equip and supply the ship.

(*c*) Make the holds, refrigerating and cool chambers, and all other parts of the ship in which goods are carried, fit and safe for their reception, carriage and preservation.

2. Subject to the provisions of Article IV, the carrier shall properly and carefully load, handle, stow, carry, keep, care for, and discharge the goods carried.

3. After receiving the goods into his charge the carrier or the master or agent of the carrier shall, on demand of the shipper, issue to the shipper a bill of lading showing among other things:

(*a*) The leading marks necessary for identification of the goods as the same are furnished in writing by the shipper before the loading of such goods starts, provided such marks are stamped or otherwise shown clearly upon the goods if uncovered, or on the cases or coverings in which such goods are contained, in such a manner as should ordinarily remain legible until the end of the voyage.

(*b*) Either the number of packages or pieces, or the quantity, or weight, as the case may be, as furnished in writing by the shipper.

(*c*) The apparent order and condition of the goods.

Provided that no carrier, master or agent of the carrier shall be bound to state or show in the bill of lading any marks, number, quantity, or weight which he has reasonable ground for suspecting not accurately to represent the goods actually received, or which he has had no reasonable means of checking.

4. Such a bill of lading shall be prima facie evidence of the receipt by the carrier of the goods as therein described in accordance with paragraph 3(*a*), (*b*) and (*c*). However, proof to the contrary shall not be admissible when the bill of lading has been transferred to a third party acting in good faith.

5. The shipper shall be deemed to have guaranteed to the carrier the accuracy at the time of shipment of the marks, number, quantity and weight, as furnished by him, and the shipper shall indemnify the carrier against all loss, damages and expenses arising or resulting from inaccuracies in such particulars. The right of the carrier to such indemnity shall in no

way limit his responsibility and liability under the contract of carriage to any person other than the shipper.

6. Unless notice of loss or damage and the general nature of such loss or damage be given in writing to the carrier or his agent at the port of discharge before or at the time of the removal of the goods into the custody of the person entitled to delivery thereof under the contract of carriage, or, if the loss or damage be not apparent, within three days, such removal shall be prima facie evidence of the delivery by the carrier of the goods as described in the bill of lading.

The notice in writing need not be given if the state of the goods has, at the time of their receipt, been the subject of joint survey or inspection.

Subject to parabraph 6 *bis* the carrier and the ship shall in any event be discharged from all liability whatsoever in respect of the goods, unless suit is brought within one year of their delivery or of the date when they should have been delivered. This period may, however, be extended if the parties so agree after the cause of action has arisen.

In the case of any actual or apprehended loss or damage the carrier and the receiver shall give all reasonable facilities to each other for inspecting and tallying the goods.

6 *bis*. An action for indemnity against a third person may be brought even after the expiration of the year provided for in the preceding paragraph if brought within the time allowed by the law of the Court seized of the case. However, the time allowed shall be not less than three months, commencing from the day when the person bringing such action for indemnity has settled the claim or has been served with process in the action against himself.

7. After the goods are loaded the bill of lading to be issued by the carrier, master, or agent of the carrier, to the shipper shall, if the shipper so demands, be a 'shipped' bill of lading, provided that if the shipper shall have previously taken up any document of title to such goods, he shall surrender the same as against the issue of the 'shipped' bill of lading, but at the option of the carrier such document of title may be noted at the port of shipment by the carrier, master, or agent with the name or names of the ship or ships upon which the goods have been shipped and the date or dates of shipment, and when so noted, if it shows the particulars mentioned in paragraph 3 of Article III, shall for the purpose of this article be deemed to constitute a 'shipped' bill of lading.

8. Any clause, covenant, or agreement in a contract of carriage relieving the carrier or the ship from liability for loss or damage to, or in connection with, goods arising from negligence, fault, or failure in the duties and obligations provided in this article or lessening such liability otherwise than as provided in these Rules, shall be null and void and of no effect. A benefit of insurance in favour of the carrier or similar clause shall be deemed to be a clause relieving the carrier from liability.

Article IV

1. Neither the carrier nor the ship shall be liable for loss or damage arising or resulting from unseaworthiness unless caused by want of due diligence on the part of the carrier to make the ship seaworthy, and to secure that the ship is properly manned, equipped and supplied, and to make the holds, refrigerating and cool chambers and all other parts of the ship in which goods are carried fit and safe for their reception, carriage and preservation in accordance with the provision of paragraph 1 of Article III. Whenever loss or damage has resulted from unseaworthiness the burden of proving the exercise of due diligence shall be on the carrier or other person claiming exemption under this article.

2. Neither the carrier nor the ship shall be responsible for loss or damage arising or resulting from:

(*a*) Act, neglect, or default of the master, mariner, pilot, or the servants of the carrier in the navigation or in the management of the ship.

(*b*) Fire, unless caused by the actual fault or privity of the carrier.

(*c*) Perils, dangers and accidents of the sea or other navigable waters.

(*d*) Act of God.

(*e*) Act of war.

(*f*) Act of public enemies.

(*g*) Arrest or restraint of princes, rulers or people, or seizure under legal process.

(*h*) Quarantine restrictions.

(*i*) Act or omission of the shipper or owner of the goods, his agent or representative.

(*j*) Strikes or lockouts or stoppage or restraint of labour from whatever cause, whether partial or general.

(*k*) Riots and civil commotions.

(*l*) Saving or attempting to save life or property at sea.

(*m*) Wastage in bulk or weight or any other loss or damage arising from inherent defect, quality or vice of the goods.

(*n*) Insufficiency of packing.

(*o*) Insufficiency or inadequacy of marks.

(*p*) Latent defects not discoverable by due diligence.

(*q*) Any other cause arising without the actual fault or privity of the carrier, or without the fault or neglect of the agents or servants of the carrier, but the burden of proof shall be on the person claiming the benefit of this exception to show that neither the actual fault or privity of the carrier nor the fault or neglect of the agents or servants of the carrier contributed to the loss or damage.

3. The shipper shall not be responsible for loss or damage sustained by the carrier or the ship arising or resulting from any cause without the act, fault or neglect of the shipper, his agents or his servants.

4. Any deviation in saving or attempting to save life or property at sea or any reasonable deviation shall not be deemed to be an infringement or

breach of these Rules or of the contract of carriage, and the carrier shall not be liable for any loss or damage resulting therefrom.

5. (a) Unless the nature and value of such goods have been declared by the shipper before shipment and inserted in the bill of lading, neither the carrier nor the ship shall in any event be or become liable for any loss or damage to or in connection with the goods in an amount exceeding the equivalent of 10,000 francs per package or unit or 30 francs per kilo of gross weight of the goods lost or damaged, whichever is the higher.

(b) The total amount recoverable shall be calculated by reference to the value of such goods at the place and time at which the goods are discharged from the ship in accordance with the contract or should have been so discharged.

The value of the goods shall be fixed according to the commodity exchange price, or, if there be no such price, according to the current market price, or, if there be no commodity exchange price or current market price, by reference to the normal value of goods of the same kind and quality.

(c) Where a container, pallet or similar article of transport is used to consolidate goods, the number of packages or units enumerated in the bill of lading as packed in such article of transport shall be deemed the number of packages or units for the purpose of this paragraph as far as these packages or units are concerned. Except as aforesaid such article of transport shall be considered the package or unit.

(d) A franc means a unit consisting of 65.5 milligrammes of gold of millesimal fineness 900. The date of conversion of the sum awarded into national currencies shall be governed by the law of the Court seized of the case.

(e) Neither the carrier nor the ship shall be entitled to the benefit of the limitation of liability provided for in this paragraph if it is proved that the damage resulted from an act or omission of the carrier done with intent to cause damage, or recklessly and with knowledge that damage would probably result.

(f) The declaration mentioned in sub-paragraph (a) of this paragraph, if embodied in the bill of lading, shall be prima facie evidence, but shall not be binding or conclusive on the carrier.

(g) By agreement between the carrier, master or agent of the carrier and the shipper other maximum amounts than those mentioned in sub-paragraph (a) of this paragraph may be fixed, provided that no maximum amount so fixed shall be less than the appropriate maximum mentioned in that sub-paragraph.

(h) Neither the carrier nor the ship shall be responsible in any event for loss or damage to, or in connection with, goods if the nature or value thereof has been knowingly mis-stated by the shipper in the bill of lading.

6. Goods of an inflammable, explosive or dangerous nature to the shipment whereof the carrier, master or agent of the carrier has not consented with knowledge of their nature and character, may at any time

before discharge be landed at any place, or destroyed or rendered innocuous by the carrier without compensation and the shipper of such goods shall be liable for all damages and expenses directly or indirectly arising out of or resulting from such shipment. If any such goods shipped with such knowledge and consent shall become a danger to the ship or cargo, they may in like manner be landed at any place, or destroyed or rendered innocuous by the carrier without liability on the part of the carrier except to general average, if any.

Article IV bis

1. The defences and limits of liability provided for in these Rules shall apply in any action against the carrier in respect of loss or damage to goods covered by a contract of carriage whether the action be founded in contract or in tort.

2. If such an action is brought against a servant or agent of the carrier (such servant or agent not being an independent contractor), such servants or agent shall be entitled to avail himself of the defences and limits of liability which the carrier is entitled to invoke under these Rules.

3. The aggregate of the amounts recoverable from the carrier, and such servants and agents, shall in no case exceed the limit provided for in these Rules.

4. Nevertheless, a servant or agent of the carrier shall not be entitled to avail himself of the provision of this article, if it is proved that the damage resulted from an act or omission of the servant or agent done with intent to cause damage or recklessly and with knowledge that damage would probably result.

Article V

A carrier shall be at liberty to surrender in whole or in part all or any of his rights and immunities or to increase any of his responsibilities and obligations under these Rules, provided such surrender or increase shall be embodied in the bill of lading issued to the shipper. The provisions of these Rules shall not be applicable to charter parties, but if bills of lading are issued in the case of a ship under a charter party they shall comply with the terms of these Rules. Nothing in these Rules shall be held to prevent the insertion in a bill of lading of any lawful provision regarding general average.

Article VI

Notwithstanding the provisions of the preceding articles, a carrier, master or agent of the carrier and a shipper shall in regard to any particular goods be at liberty to enter into any agreement in any terms as to the responsibility and liability of the carrier for such goods, and as to the rights and immunities of the carrier in respect of such goods, or his obligation as to seaworthiness, so far as this stipulation is not contrary to public policy, or the care or diligence of his servants or agents in regard to the loading, handling, stowage, carriage, custody, care and discharge of the goods carried by sea, provided that in this case no bill of lading has been or shall be issued and that the terms agreed shall be embodied in a receipt which shall be a non-negotiable document and shall be marked as such.

Any agreement so entered into shall have full legal effect.

Provided that this article shall not apply to ordinary commercial shipments made in the ordinary course of trade, but only to other shipments where the character or condition of the property to be carried or the circumstances, terms and conditions under which the carriage is to be performed are such as reasonably to justify a special agreement.

Article VII

Nothing herein contained shall prevent a carrier or a shipper from entering into any agreement, stipulation, condition, reservation or exemption as to the responsibility and liability of the carrier or the ship for the loss or damage to, or in connection with, the custody and care and handling of goods prior to the loading on, and subsequent to the discharge from, the ship on which the goods are carried by sea.

Article VIII

The provisions of these Rules shall not affect the rights and obligations of the carrier under any statute for the time being in force relating to the limitation of the liability of owners of sea-going vessels.

Article IX

These Rules shall not affect the provisions of any international Convention or national law governing liability for nuclear damage.

Article X

The provisions of these Rules shall apply to every bill of lading relating to the carriage of goods between ports in two different States if:

(a) the bill of lading is issued in a contracting State,

or

(b) The carriage is from a port in a contracting State,

or

(c) the contract contained in or evidenced by the bill of lading provides that these Rules or legislation of any State giving effect to them are to govern the contract,

whatever may be the nationality of the ship, the carrier, the shipper, the consignee, or any other interested person.

Appendix B York-Antwerp Rules

The Rules adopted by the International Maritime Committee at the Hamburg Conference of April 1974

York-Antwerp Rules 1974	*York-Antwerp Rules 1950*
Rule of Interpretation In the adjustment of general average the following lettered and numbered Rules shall apply to the exclusion of any Law and Practice inconsistent therewith. Except as provided by the numbered Rules, general averages shall be adjusted according to the lettered Rules.	**Rule of Interpretation** – Same
Rule A There is a general average act when, and only when, any extraordinary sacrifice or expenditure is intentionally and reasonably made or incurred for the common safety for the purpose of preserving from peril the property involved in a common maritime adventure.	**Rule A** – Same
Rule B General average sacrifices and expenses shall be borne by the different contributing interests on the basis hereinafter provided.	**Rule B** – Same
Rule C Only such losses, damages or expenses which are the direct consequence of the general average act shall be allowed as general average. Loss or damage sustained by the ship or cargo through delay, whether on the voyage or subsequently, such as demurrage, and any indirect loss whatsoever, such as loss of market, shall not be admitted as general average.	**Rule C** – Same

146

York-Antwerp Rules 1974

York-Antwerp Rules 1950

Rule D
Rights to contribution in general average shall not be affected, though the event which gave rise to the sacrifice or expenditure may have been due to the fault of one of the parties to the adventure, but this shall not prejudice any remedies or defences which may be open against or to that party in respect of such fault.

Rule D
Rights to contribution in general average shall not be affected, though the event which gave rise to the sacrifice or expenditure may have been due to the fault of one of the parties to the adventure; but this shall not prejudice any remedies which may be open against that party for such fault.

Rule E
The onus of proof is upon the party claiming in general average to show that the loss or expense claimed is properly allowable as general average.

Rule E — Same

Rule F
Any extra expense incurred in place of another expense which would have been allowable as general average shall be deemed to be general average and so allowed without regard to the saving, if any, to other interests, but only up to the amount of the general average expense avoided.

Rule F — Same

Rule G
General average shall be adjusted as regards both loss and contribution upon the basis of values at the time and place when and where the adventure ends.

This rule shall not affect the determination of the place at which the average statement is to be made up.

Rule G — Same

Rule I — Jettison of Cargo
No jettison of cargo shall be made good as general average, unless such cargo is carried in accordance with the recognized custom of the trade.

Rule I — Same

Rule II — Damage by Jettison and Sacrifice for the Common Safety
Damage done to a ship and cargo, or either of them, by or in consequence of a sacrifice made for the common safety, and by water which goes down a ship's hatches opened or other opening made for the purpose of making a jettison for the common safety, shall be made good as general average.

Rule II — Same

York-Antwerp Rules 1974

York-Antwerp Rules 1950

Rule III — Extinguishing Fire on Shipboard
Damage done to a ship and cargo, or either of them, by water or otherwise, including damage by beaching or scuttling a burning ship, in extinguishing a fire on board the ship, shall be made good as general average; except that no compensation shall be made for damage by smoke or heat however caused.

Rule III — Extinguishing Fire on Shipboard
Damage done to a ship and cargo, or either of them, by water or otherwise, including damage by beaching or scuttling a burning ship, in extinguishing a fire on board the ship, shall be made good as general average; except that no compensation shall be made for damage to such portions of the ship and bulk cargo, or to such separate packages or cargo, as have been on fire.

Rule IV — Cutting away Wreck
Loss or damage sustained by cutting away wreck or parts of the ship which have been previously carried away or are effectively lost by accident shall not be made good as general average.

Rule IV — Cutting away Wreck
Loss or damage caused by cutting away the wreck or remains of spars, or of other things which have previously been carried away by sea peril, shall not be made good as general average.

Rule V — Voluntary Stranding
When a ship is intentionally run on shore for the common safety, whether or not she might have been driven on shore, the consequent loss or damage shall be allowed in general average.

Rule V — Voluntary Stranding
When a ship is intentionally run on shore, and the circumstances are such that if that course were not adopted she would inevitably drive on shore or on rocks, no loss or damage caused to the ship, cargo and freight or any of them by such intentional running on shore shall be made good as general average, but loss or damage incurred in refloating such a ship shall be allowed as general average.

In all other cases where a ship is intentionally run on shore for the common safety, the consequent loss or damage shall be allowed as general average.

Rule VI — Salvage Remuneration
Expenditure incurred by the parties to the adventure on account of salvage, whether under contract or otherwise, shall be allowed in general average to the extent that the salvage operations were undertaken for the purpose of preserving from peril the property involved in the common maritime adventure.

Rule VI — Carrying Press of Sail — Damage to or Loss of Sails
Damage to or loss of sails and spars or either of them, caused by forcing a ship off the ground or by driving her higher up the ground, for the common safety, shall be made good as general average; but where a ship is afloat, no loss or damage caused to the ship, cargo and freight, or any of them, by carrying a press of sail, shall be made good as general average.

(*Note:* this Rule has been deleted as

being absolete and a new Rule VI on the subject of salvage remuneration has been substituted at this point in order to preserve the numbering of the Rules.)

Rule VII—Damage to Machinery and Boilers
Damage caused to any machinery and boilers of a ship which is ashore and in a position of peril, in endeavouring to refloat, shall be allowed in general average when shown to have arisen from an actual intention to float the ship for the common safety at the risk of such damage; but where a ship is afloat no loss or damage caused by working the propelling machinery and boilers shall in any circumstances be made good as general average.

Rule VII—Damage to Machinery and Boilers
Damage caused to machinery and boilers of a ship which is ashore and in a position of peril, in endeavouring to refloat, shall be allowed in general average when shown to have arisen from an actual intention to float the ship for the common safety at the risk of such damage; but where a ship is afloat no loss or damage caused by working the machinery and boilers, including loss or damage due to compounding of engines or such measures, shall in any circumstances be made good as general average.

Rule VIII—Expenses Lightening a Ship when Ashore, and Consequent Damage
When a ship is ashore and cargo and ship's fuel and stores or any of them are discharged as a general average act, the extra cost of lightening, lighter hire and reshipping if incurred and the loss or damage sustained thereby, shall be admitted as general average.

Rule VIII—Same

Rule IX—Ship's Materials and Stores Burnt for Fuel
Ship's materials and stores, or any of them, necessarily burnt for fuel for the common safety at a time of peril, shall be admitted as general average, when and only when an ample supply of fuel had been provided; but the estimated quantity of fuel that would have been consumed, calculated at the price current at the ship's last port of departure at the date of her leaving, shall be credited to the general average.

Rule IX—Same

Rule X—Expenses at Port of Refuge, etc
(*a*) When a ship shall have entered a port or place of refuge, or shall have returned

Rule X—Expenses at Port of Refuge, etc
(*a*) When a ship shall have entered a port or place of refuge, or shall have returned

York-Antwerp Rules 1974

to her port or place of loading in consequence of accident, sacrifice or other extraordinary circumstances, which render that necessary for the common safety, the expenses of entering such port or place shall be admitted as general average; and when she shall have sailed thence with her original cargo, or a part of it, the corresponding expenses of leaving such port or place consequent upon such entry or return shall likewise be admitted as general average.

When a ship is at any port or place of refuge and is necessarily removed to another port or place because repairs cannot be carried out in the first port or place, the provisions of this Rule shall be applied to the second port or place as if it were a port or place of refuge and the cost of such removal including temporary repairs and towage shall be admitted as general average. The provisions of Rule XI shall be applied to the prolongation of the voyage occasioned by such removal.

(*b*) The cost of handling on board or discharging cargo, fuel or stores whether at a port or place of loading, call or refuge shall be admitted as general average, when the handling or discharge was necessary for the common safety or to enable damage to the ship caused by sacrifice or accident to be repaired, if the repairs were necessary for the safe prosecution of the voyage, except in cases where the damage to the ship is discovered at a port or place of loading or call without any accident or other extraordinary circumstances connected with such damage having taken place during the voyage.

The cost of handling on board or discharging cargo, fuel or stores shall not be admissible as general average when incurred solely for the purpose of restowage due to shifting during the voyage unless such re-stowage is necessary for the common safety.

York-Antwerp Rules 1950

to her port or place of loading in consequence of accident, sacrifice or other extraordinary circumstances, which render that necessary for the common safety, the expenses of entering such port or place shall be admitted as general average; and when she shall have sailed thence with her original cargo, or a part of it, the corresponding expenses of leaving such port or place consequent upon such entry or return shall likewise be admitted as general average.

When a ship is at any port or place of refuge and is necessarily removed to another port or place because repairs cannot be carried out in the first port or place, the provisions of this Rule shall be applied to the second port or place as if it were a port or place of refuge. The provisions of Rule XI shall be applied to the prolongation of the voyage occasioned by such removal.

(*b*) The cost of handling on board or discharging cargo, fuel or stores whether at a port or place of loading, call or refuge, shall be admitted as general average when the handling or discharge was necessary for the common safety or to enable damage to the ship caused by sacrifice or accident to be repaired, if the repairs were necessary for the safe prosecution of the voyage.

York-Antwerp Rules 1974

(*c*) Whenever the cost of handling or discharging cargo, fuel or stores is admissible as general average, the costs of storage, including insurance if reasonably incurred, reloading and stowing of such cargo, fuel or stores shall likewise be admitted as general average.

But when the ship is condemned or does not proceed on her original voyage storage expenses shall be admitted as general average only up to the date of the ship's condemnation or of the abandonment of the voyage or up to the date of completion of discharge of cargo if the condemnation or abandonment takes place before that date.

(*Note:* there is no intention to change the substance of rules X(*c*). The revision is made purely in the interest of economy of words.)

(*d*) Deleted

Rule XI—Wages and Maintenance of Crew and other expenses bearing up for and in a Port of Refuge, etc.
(*a*) Wages and Maintenance of masters, officers and crew reasonably incurred and fuel and stores consumed during the prolongation of the voyage occasioned by a ship entering a port or place of refuge or returning to her port or place of loading shall be admitted as general average when the expenses of entering

York-Antwerp Rules 1950

(*c*) Whenever the cost of handling or discharging cargo, fuel or stores is admissible as general average, the cost of reloading and stowing such cargo, fuel or stores on board the ship, together with all storage charges (including insurance, if reasonably incurred) on such cargo, fuel or stores, shall likewise be so admitted. But when the ship is condemned or does not proceed on her original voyage, no storage expenses incurred after the date of the ship's condemnation or of the abandonment of the voyage shall be admitted as general average. In the event of the condemnation of the ship or the abandonment of the voyage before completion of discharge of cargo, storage expenses, as above, shall be admitted as general average up to the date of completion of discharge.

(*d*) If a ship under average be in a port or place at which it is practicable to repair her, so as to enable her to carry on the whole cargo, and if, in order to save expense, either she is towed thence to some other port of repair or to her destination, or the cargo or a portion of it is transhipped by another ship, or otherwise forwarded, then the extra cost of such towage, transhipment and forwarding, or any of them (up to the amount of the extra expense saved) shall be payable by the several parties to the adventure in proportion to the extraordinary expense saved.

Rule XI—Wages and Maintenance of Crew and other Expenses bearing up for and in a Port of Refuge, etc.
(*a*) Wages and maintenance of master, officers and crew reasonably incurred and fuel and stores consumed during the prolongation of the voyage occasioned by a ship entering a port or place of refuge or returning to her port or place of loading, shall be admitted as general average when the expenses of entering

York-Antwerp Rules 1974

York-Antwerp Rules 1950

such port or place are allowable in general average in accordance with Rule X(*a*).

(*b*) When a ship shall have entered or been detained in any port or place in consequence of accident, sacrifice or other extraordinary circumstances which render that necessary for the common safety, or to enable damage to the ship caused by sacrifice or accident to be repaired, if the repairs were necessary for the safe prosecution of the voyage, the wages and maintenance of the master, officers, and crew reasonably incurred during the extra period of detention in such port or place until the ship shall or should have been made ready to proceed upon her voyage, shall be admitted in general average.

Provided that when damage to the ship is discovered at a port or place of loading or call without any accident or other extraordinary circumstance connected with such damage having taken place during the voyage, then the wages and maintenance of master, officers and crew and fuel and stores consumed during the extra detention for repairs to damages to discovered shall not be admissible as general average, even if the repairs are necessary for the safe prosecution of the voyage.

When the ship is condemned or does not proceed on her original voyage, wages and maintenance of the master, officers and crew and fuel and stores consumed shall be admitted as general average only up to the date of the ship's condemnation or of the abandonment of the voyage or up to the date of completion of discharge of cargo if the condemnation or abandonment takes place before that date.

(*Note:* this revision follows the revised wording of Rule X(*c*).)

Fuel and stores consumed during the extra period of detention shall be

such port or place are allowable in general average in accordance with Rule X(*a*).

(*b*) When a ship shall have entered or been detained in any port or place on consequence of accident, sacrifice or other extraordinary circumstances which render that necessary for the common safety, or to enable damage to the ship caused by sacrifice or accident to be repaired, if the repairs were necessary for the safe prosecution of the voyage, the wages and maintenance of the master, officers and crew reasonably incurred during the extra period of detention in such port or place until the ship shall or should have been made ready to proceed upon her voyage, shall be admitted in general average. When the ship is condemned or does not proceed on her original voyage, the extra period of detention shall be deemed not to extend beyond the date of the ship's condemnation or of the abandonment of the voyage or, if discharge of cargo is not then completed, beyond the date of completion of discharge.

Fuel and stores consumed during the extra period of detention shall be admitted as general average, except such fuel and stores as are consumed in effecting repairs not allowable in general average.

Port charges incurred during the extra period of detention shall likewise be admitted as general average except such charges as are incurred solely by reason of repairs not allowable in general average.

admitted as general average, except such fuel and stores as are consumed in effecting repairs not allowable in general average.

Port charges incurred during the extra period of detention shall likewise be admitted as general average except such charges as are incurred solely by reason of repairs not allowable in general average.

(*c*) For the purpose of this and the other Rules wages shall include all payments made to or for the benefit of the master, officers and crew, whether such payments be imposed by law upon the shipowners or be made under the terms of articles of employment.

(*d*) When overtime is paid to the master, officers or crew for maintenance of the ship or repairs, the cost of which is not allowable in general average, such overtime shall be allowed in general average only up to the saving in expense which would have been incurred and admitted as general average, had such overtime not been incurred.

Rule XII—Damage to Cargo in Discharging etc.
Damage to or loss of cargo, fuel or stores caused in the act of handling, discharging, storing, reloading and stowing shall be made good as general average, when and only when the cost of those measures respectively is admitted as general average.

Rules XIII—Deductions from Cost of Repairs
Repairs to be allowed in general average shall not be subject to deduction in respect of 'new for old' where old material or parts are replaced by new unless the ship is over fifteen years old in which case there shall be a deduction of one-third. The deductions shall be

(*c*) For the purpose of this and the other Rules wages shall include all payments made to or for the benefit of the master, officers or crew, whether such payments be imposed by law upon the shipowners or be made under the terms or articles of employment.

(*d*) When overtime is paid to the master, officers or crew for maintenance of the ship or repairs, the cost of which is not allowable in general average, such overtime shall be allowed in general average only up to the saving in expense which would have been incurred and admitted as general average had such overtime not been incurred.

Rule XII—Same

Rules XIII—Deductions from Cost of Repairs
In adjusting claims for general average, repairs to be allowed in general average shall be subject to deductions in respect of 'new for old' according to the following rules, where old material or parts are replaced by new.

The deductions to be regulated by

regulated by the age of the ship from 31 December of the year of completion of construction to the date of the general average act, except for insulation, life and similar boats, communications and navigational apparatus and equipment, machinery and boilers for which deductions shall be regulated by the age of the particular parts to which they apply.

The deductions shall be made only from the cost of the new material or parts when finished and ready to be installed in the ship.

No deduction shall be made in respect of provisions, stores, anchors and chain cables.

Drydock and slipway dues and costs of shifting the ship shall be allowed in full.

The costs of cleaning, painting or coating of bottom shall not be allowed in general average unless the bottom has been painted or coated within the twelve months preceding the date of the general average act in which case one half of such costs shall be allowed.

the age of the ship from date or original register to the date of accident, except for provisions and stores, insulation, life- and similar boats, gyro compass equipment, wireless, direction finding, echo sounding and similar apparatus, machinery and boilers for which the deductions shall be regulated by the age of the particular parts to which they apply.

No deduction to be made in respect of provisions, stores and gear which have not been in use.

The deductions shall be made from the cost of new material or parts, including labour and establishment charges, but excluding cost of opening up.

Drydock and slipway dues and costs of shifting the ship shall be allowed in full.

No cleaning and painting of bottom to be allowed, if the bottom has not been painted within six months previous to the date of the accident.

A. Up to 1 year old
All repairs to be allowed in full, except scaling and cleaning and painting or coating of bottom, from which one-third is to be deducted.

B. Between 1 and 3 years old
Deductions of scaling, cleaning and painting bottom as above under Clause A.

One-third to be deducted off sails, rigging, ropes, sheets and hawsers (other than wire and chain), awnings, covers, provisions and stores and painting.

One-sixth to be deducted off woodwork of hull, including hold ceiling, wooden masts, spars and boats, furniture, upholstery, crockery, metal and glassware, wire rigging, wire ropes and wire hawsers, gyro compass equipment, wireless, direction finding, echo sounding and similar apparatus, chain cables and chains, insulation, auxiliary machinery, steering gear and connections, winches and cranes and connections and electrical machinery and connections other than electrical propelling machinery; other repairs to be allowed in full.

Metal sheathing for wooden or composite ships shall be dealt with by allowing in full the cost of a weight equal to the gross weight of metal sheathing stripped off, minus the proceeds of the old metal. Nails, felt and labour metalling are subject to a deduction of one-third.

C. Between 3 and 6 years
Deductions as above under clause B, except that one-third be deducted off woodwork of hull including hold ceiling, wooden masts, spars and boats, furniture, upholstery, and one-sixth be deducted off iron work of masts and spars and all machinery (inclusive of boilers and their mountings).

D. Between 6 and 10 years
Deductions as above under Clause C, except that one-third be deducted off all rigging, ropes, sheets, and hawsers, iron work of masts and spars, gyro compass equipment, wireless, direction finding, echo sounding and similar apparatus, insulation, auxiliary machinery, steering gear, winches, cranes and connections and all other machinery (inclusive of boilers and their mountings).

E. Between 10 and 15 years
One-third to be deducted off all renewals except iron work of hull and cementing and chain cables, from which one-sixth to be deducted, and anchors which are allowed in full.

F. Over 15 years
One-third to be deducted off all renewals, except chain cables, from which one-sixth to be deducted and anchors, which are allowed in full.

Rule XIV — Temporary Repairs
Where temporary repairs are effected to a ship at a port of loading, call or refuge, for common safety, or of damage caused by general average sacrifice, the cost of such repairs shall be admitted as general average.

Rule XIV — Temporary Repairs
Where temporary repairs are effected to a ship at a port of loading, call or refuge, for the common safety, or of damage caused by general average sacrifice, the cost of such repairs shall be admitted as general average.

York-Antwerp Rules 1974	*York-Antwerp Rules 1950*
Where temporary repairs of accidental damage are effected in order to enable the adventure to be completed, the cost of such repairs shall be admitted as general average without regard to the saving, if any, to other interests, but only up to the saving in expense which would have been incurred and allowed in general average if such repairs had not been effected there.	Where temporary repairs of accidental damage are effected merely to enable the adventure to be completed, the cost of such repairs shall be admitted as general average without regard to the saving, if any, to other interests, but only up to the saving in expense which would have been incurred and allowed in general average, if such repairs had not been effected there.
No deductions 'new for old' shall be made from the cost of temporary repairs allowable as general average.	No deductions 'new for old' shall be made from the cost of temporary repairs allowable as general average.

Rule XV—Loss of Freight

Loss of Freight arising from damage to or loss of cargo shall be made good as general average, either when caused by a general average act, or when the damage to or loss of cargo is so made good.

Deduction shall be made from the amount of gross freight lost, of the charges which the owner thereof would have incurred to earn such freight, but has, in consequence of the sacrifice, not incurred.

Rule XV—Same

Rule XVI—Amount to be made good for Cargo Lost or Damaged by Sacrifice

The amount to be made good as General Average for damage to or loss of cargo sacrificed shall be the loss which has been sustained thereby based on the value at the time of discharge, ascertained from the commercial invoice rendered to the receiver or if there is no such invoice from the shipped value. The value at the time of discharge shall include the cost of insurance and freight except insofar as such freight is at the risk of interests other than the cargo.

When cargo so damaged is sold and the amount of the damage has not been otherwise agreed, the loss to be made good in general average shall be the difference between the net proceeds of sale and the net sound value as computed in the first paragraph of this Rule.

Rule XVI—Amount to be made good for Cargo Lost or Damaged by Sacrifice

The amount to be made good as general average for damage to or loss of goods sacrificed shall be the loss which the owner of the goods has sustained thereby, based on the market values at the last day of discharge of the vessels or at the termination of the adventure where this ends at a place other than the original destination.

Where goods so damaged are sold and the amount of the damage has not been otherwise agreed, the loss to be made good in general average shall be the difference between the net proceeds of sale and the net sound value at the last day of discharge of the vessel or at the termination of the adventure where this ends at a place other than the original destination.

York-Antwerp Rules 1974

Rule XVII—Contributory Values
The contribution to a general average shall be made upon the actual net values of the property at the termination of the adventure except that the value of cargo shall be the value at the time of discharge ascertained from the commercial invoice rendered to the receiver or if there is no such invoice from the shipped value. The value of the cargo shall include the cost of insurance and freight unless and insofar as such freight is at the risk of interests other than the cargo, deducting therefrom any loss or damage suffered by the cargo prior to or at the time of discharge. The value of the ship shall be assessed without taking into account the beneficial or detrimental effect of any demise or time charter party to which the ship may be committed.

To these values shall be added the amount made good as general average for property sacrificed, if not already included, deduction being made from the freight and passage money at risk of such charges and crew's wages as would not have been incurred in earning the freight had the ship and cargo been totally lost at the date of the general average act and have not been allowed as general average; deduction being also made from the value of the property of all extra charges incurred in respect thereof subsequently to the general average act, except such charges as are allowed in general average.

Where cargo is sold short of destination, however, it shall contribute upon the actual net proceeds of sale, with the addition of any amount made good as general average.

Passenger's luggage and personal effects not shipped under Bill of Lading shall not contribute in general average.

Rule XVIII—Damage to Ship
The amount to be allowed as general average for damage or loss to the ship, her machinery and/or gear caused by a general average act shall be as follows:

York-Antwerp Rules 1950

Rule XVII—Contributory Values
The contribution to a general average shall be made upon the actual net values of the property at the termination of the adventure, to which values shall be added the amount made good as general average for property sacrificed, if not already included, deduction being made from the shipowner's freight and passage money at risk, of such charges and crew's wages as would not have been incurred in earning the freight had the ship and cargo been totally lost at the date of the general average act and have not been allowed as general average; deduction being also made from the value of the property of all charges incurred in respect thereof subsequently to the general average act, except such charges as are allowed in general average.

Passengers' luggage and personal effects not shipped under bill of lading shall not contribute in general average.

Rule XVIII—Damage to Ship
The amount to be allowed as general average for damage or loss to the ship, her machinery and/or gear when repaired or replaced shall be the actual reasonable

York-Antwerp Rules 1974

York-Antwerp Rules 1950

(*a*) When repaired or replaced, the actual reasonable cost of repairing or replacing such damage or loss, subject to deduction in accordance with Rule XIII.

(*b*) When not repaired or replaced, the reasonable depreciation arising from such damage or loss, but not exceeding the estimated cost of repairs. But where the ship is an actual total loss or when the cost of repairs of the damage would exceed the value of the ship when repaired, the amount to be allowed as general average shall be the difference between the estimated sound value of the ship after deducting therefrom the estimated cost of repairing damage which is not general average and the value of the ship in her damaged state which may be measured by the net proceeds of sale, if any.

cost of repairing or replacing such damage or loss, subject to deduction in accordance with Rule XIII. When not repaired, the reasonable depreciation shall be allowed, not exceeding the estimated cost of repairs.

Where there is an actual or constructive total loss of the ship, the amount to be allowed as general average for damage or loss to the ship caused by a general average act shall be the estimated sound value of the ship after deducting therefrom the estimated cost of repairing damage which is not general average and the proceeds of sale, if any.

Rule XIX—Undeclared or Wrongfully Declared Cargo
Damage or loss caused to goods loaded without the knowledge of the shipowner or his agent or to goods wilfully misdescribed at time of shipment shall not be allowed as general average, but such goods shall remain liable to contribute, if saved.

Damage or loss caused to goods which have been wrongfully declared on shipment at a value which is lower than their real value shall be contributed for at the declared value, but such goods shall contribute upon their actual value.

Rule XIX—Same

Rule XX—Provision of Funds
A commission of 2 per cent on general average disbursements, other than the wages and maintenance of master, officers and crew and fuel and stores not replaced during the voyage, shall be allowed in general average, but when the funds are not provided by any of the contributing interests, the necessary cost of obtaining the funds required by means of a bottomry bond or otherwise, or the

Rule XX—Same

loss sustained by owners of goods sold for the purpose, shall be allowed in general average.

The cost of insuring money advanced to pay for general average disbursements shall also be allowed in general average.

Rule XXI—Interest on Losses made good in General Average
Interest shall be allowed on expenditure, sacrifices and allowances charged to general average at the rate of 7 per cent per annum, until the date of the general average statement, due allowance being made for any interim reimbursement from the contributory interests or from the general average deposit fund.

Rule XXII—Treatment of Cash Deposits
Where cash deposits have been collected in respect of cargo's liability for general average, salvage or special charges, such deposits shall be paid without any delay into a special account in the joint names of a representative nominated on behalf of the shipowner and a representative nominated on behalf of the depositors in a bank to be approved by both. The sum so deposited, together with accrued interest, if any, shall be held as security for payment to the parties entitled thereto of the general average, salvage or special charges payable by cargo in respect to which the deposits have been collected. Payments on account of refund of deposits may be made if certified to in writing by the average adjuster. Such deposits and payments or refunds shall be without prejudice to the ultimate liability of the parties.

Rule XXI—Interest on Losses made good in General Average
Interest shall be allowed on expenditure, sacrifices and allowances charged to general average at the rate of 5 per cent per annum, until the date of the general average statement, due allowance being made for any interim reimbursement from the contributory interests or from the general average deposit fund.

Rule XXII—Same

Appendix C Lloyd's Bottomry Bond

The following is the form of Lloyd's Bottomry Bond—

KNOW ALL MEN BY THESE PRESENTS
   that I
   Master of the Ship
   of the Port of
   of the burthen of

                          tons or thereabouts, am held
and firmly bound unto
of
in the sum of
sterling British money, to be repaid to the said
                         his agent, attorney, executors,
administrators, or assigns, for which payment I bind myself,
my heirs, executors, and administrators, and also bind and
hypothecate the said ship and the freight to become due in
respect of the voyage after-mentioned and the cargo laden
or to be laden on the said voyage firmly by these Presents
sealed with my seal. Dated this   day of
          19 .

This recital should be varied according to the facts.

WHEREAS the said ship lately arrived at . . . . in
distress, having sustained damages in the course of a voyage
from   to   laden with
                   and being in want of repairs,
supplies, and provisions to enable her to continue her said
voyage. AND WHEREAS the said   being
without funds or credit at   and urgently
requiring the sum of
to pay for the said repairs, supplies, and provisions and to
discharge the lawful and necessary disbursements of the ship
at   and to release her from her
liabilities, and to enable her to continue her voyage, and
having first duly communicated or attempted to communicate
with the owners of the said ship and of the said cargo with a
view to obtain funds from them, was compelled to apply for
loan upon bottomry of his ship, her cargo and freight: AND

WHEREAS the said   who is hereinafter
called the said lender, proposed and agreed to advance upon
such security the same sum of   at a maritime
premium of   per cent for the said voyage, and
the said   being unable to procure such advance
in any quarter on more advantageous terms, accepted the said
proposal [with the intervention and approval of the proper
authorities at   ], and agreed so far as he lawfully
could or might that the said security should have priority over
all other claims of the said ship, freight, and goods, whether by
himself or any other person: AND WHEREAS the said lender
has duly advanced the said sum in pursuance of the said agreement. NOW THE CONDITION of the above obligation is such
that if the said   do with the said ship
and cargo duly prosecute the said voyage without unnecessary
delay or deviation and do within   days after the
arrival of the said ship or cargo at
and before commencing to discharge or deliver her cargo there,
pay or cause to be paid to the said lender or to his order or
assigns the said sum of   together with maritime
premium thereon at the rate aforesaid, making in all the sum
of   such payment to be said at the exchange
of   for every British pound sterling or if the
said ship with the said cargo shall duly prosecute her said
voyage without unnecessary delay or deviation, and shall be by
perils of the sea lost in the course of such voyage, then his
obligation shall be null and void, and the said
shall be released from all liability in respect of the said sum
of   PROVIDED ALWAYS, and it is hereby agreed
and declared that if the said ship shall by perils of the sea as
aforesaid be lost or so much damaged as to be unable to
complete her said voyage, then if any part of the said ship or
cargo or of the said freight shall be saved or earned, the above
security, so far as regards the property saved or freight earned
shall remain in force, and the said lender or his assigns shall be
at liberty forthwith to enforce the same against such property
and freight: PROVIDED ALSO, and the said loan is made on
the express condition, that the said lender doth not accept or
take upon himself any risk or liability on the said voyage except
such as is hereby expressly mentioned, and shall not be liable
to contribute to or make good any general or particular
average loss or expenditure or other charges of a like nature
which may happen to or be sustained by or incurred in respect
of the said ship or her cargo or freight upon the said voyage in
consequence of perils of the sea or otherwise. Signed, sealed,
and delivered by the said   in the presence of

Appendix D Lloyd's Respondentia Bond

The following is the form of Lloyd's Respondentia Bond—

KNOW ALL MEN BY THESE PRESENTS
that I (*The Master of the original Ship or other person having charge of the cargo and intending to forward it*) of
am held and firmly bound unto (*the lender*)
of   in the sum of
sterling British money, to be repaid to the said
his agent, attorney, executors, administrators, or
assigns, for which payment I bind myself, my heirs, executors, and administrators, and also bind and hypothecate the cargo
of   laden or to be laden on board the ship (*Forwarding*

This recital should be varied according to the facts.
Ship) for the voyage aforementioned firmly by these presents.
Sealed with my seal   Dated this
day of   19

WHEREAS the Ship (*Original Ship*)
lately arrived at
in distress in the course of a voyage from
to   with the
above-named cargo, and the said vessel being found incapable of carrying on the said cargo the said (*the Master of the original ship or other person having charge of the cargo*)
determined in the interest of all parties concerned to forward the said cargo to its destination in the ship (*Forwarding Ship*)

(a) And/or to discharge certain liabilities in respect of which the said Cargo was subject to liens and to arrest and sale.
AND WHEREAS in order that the said cargo might be so forwarded it became necessary to provide funds to meet the expenses of discharging warehousing and reshipping the said cargo and other necessary disbursements on account of the said cargo (*a*)   AND WHEREAS
the said   being without
funds or credit at   and
urgently requiring the sum of   for the
said purposes, and having first duly communicated with or attempted to communicate with the owners of the said

162

cargo with a view to obtain funds from them, was compelled
to apply for a loan upon respondentia: AND WHEREAS the
said   who is hereinafter called the
said lender proposed and agreed to advance upon such security
the said sum of   at a maritime
premium of   per cent for the said voyage,
and the said   being unable to
procure such advance on more advantageous terms accepted
the said proposal [with the intervention and approval of the
proper authorities at   ] and agreed
so far as he lawfully could or might that the said security
should have priority over all other claims upon the said cargo,
whether by himself or any other person: AND WHEREAS the
said lender has duly advanced the said sum in pursuance of
the said agreement: NOW THE CONDITION of the above
obligation is such that if the said   do
use his best endeavours to forward or bring the said cargo to
its destination without unnecessary delay or deviation, and do
within   days after the arrival of the said cargo
at   and before the discharge or
delivery of the said cargo shall be commenced, well and truly
pay or cause to be paid to the said lender or to his order or
assigns the said sum of   together
with   the maritime
premium thereon at the rate aforesaid, making in all the sum
of   such payment to be made at the
exchange of   for every British pound
sterling, or if the said cargo shall be duly dispatched and
forwarded on the said voyage without unnecessary delay or
deviation, and the said cargo shall by perils of the sea be lost in
the course of such voyage. Then the above-written obligation
shall be null and void and the said
shall be released from all liability in respect of the said sum
of

PROVIDED ALWAYS and it is hereby agreed and declared
that if the said cargo shall in the course of the said voyage by
perils of the sea as aforesaid be lost or so much damaged as
that it cannot be carried to its said destination, then if any
part thereof shall be saved the above security, so far as regards
the property saved, shall remain in force, and the said lender
or his assigns shall be at liberty forthwith to enforce the same
against such property: PROVIDED ALSO, and the said loan
is made upon the express condition, that the said lender does
not accept or take upon himself any risk or liability on the
said voyage except such as is hereby expressly mentioned and

shall not be liable to contribute to or make good any general or particular average loss or expenditure or other charges of a like nature which may happen to or be sustained by or incurred in respect of the said cargo or the said ship upon the said voyage in consequence of perils of the sea or otherwise.

Signed, sealed and delivered by the said
in the presence of

Appendix E **Certificate of Origin**

Declaración y certificado de origen de mercaderías

Los que suscriben de profesión . . . . . . dominiciliados en . . . . . ., declaran de acuerdo con el Decreto de 31 de Diciembre de 1901 que las Mercaderías especificadas a continuación han sido embarcadas a bordo del . . . . Capitán . . . . de bandera British según conocimiento No. . . . . y proceden de los puntos que se expresan a continuación

BULTOS				Designación de la Mercadería	Cantidad en Peso o Medida Conocimiento	País de Origen de las
Marca	Nos.	Cantidad	Clase			

No. del certificado . . . . de . . . . . de 19 . . .
No. del conocimiento . . . .
    Certifico que los Señores . . . . han comprobado por medio de este certificado . . . . que las mercaderías contenidas en los . . . . bultos a que se refiere la presente Declaración son originarias de los paises mencionados en la columna correspondiente.
                        De que doy fe

Index